The Pastor as Priest

PASTORAL MINISTRY SERIES

(A series for pastors and laypeople, which addresses the nature
and scope of ministry as a task of the congregation)

The Pastor as Prophet
The Pastor as Servant
The Pastor as Priest

The Pastor as Priest

EDITED BY

Earl E. Shelp
and
Ronald H. Sunderland

The Pilgrim Press
NEW YORK

The scripture quotations are from the *Revised Standard Version of the
Bible,* copyright 1946, 1952, and © 1971, 1973 by the Division of Christian
Education, National Council of Churches, and are used by permission.

Library of Congress Cataloging-in-Publication Data

The Pastor as priest.

   (Pastoral ministry series)
   "These essays were originally presented during
the spring of 1986 as the Parker memorial lectures
in theology and ministry at the Institute of Religion
in Houston, Texas"—Acknowledgments.
   Bibliography: p. 133.
   1. Clergy—Office. 2. Priesthood. I. Shelp,
Earl E., 1947–   II. Sunderland, Ronald,
1929–   III. Title: Parker memorial lectures in
theology and ministry.   IV. Series.
BV660.2.P264   1987   262'.1   86-30430
ISBN 0-8298-0751-9 (pbk.)

The Pilgrim Press, 132 West 31 Street, New York, New York 10001

Contents

Acknowledgments

THESE ESSAYS WERE ORIGINALLY PRESENTED DURING THE spring of 1986 as the Parker Memorial Lectures in Theology and Ministry at The Institute of Religion in Houston, Texas. Funding for this third annual series of lectures was provided in loving memory of R.A. Parker by a donor who wishes to remain anonymous. Mr. Parker was a committed and tireless trustee of The Institute of Religion. His contribution to the ministry of The Institute of Religion and to the ministry of the church is perpetuated through the publication of this volume and the companion volumes in this Pastoral Ministry Series. The generosity of the individual who underwrote these lectures is gratefully acknowledged. A special word of appreciation is expressed to J. Robert Nelson, whose labors as Director of The Institute of Religion and lecturer in the third installment of the series contributed to the success of the project. Trustees of The Institute of Religion also are thanked for their interest and commitment to this aspect of the Institute's educational program. The contributors approached a difficult subject in a scholarly and practical fashion. Lolita Cannon assisted in preparing the final manuscripts for publication, and Marion M. Meyer of The Pilgrim Press shepherded the transformation of the text from manuscript to book form. To each and all, the editors express their appreciation.

Introduction

Earl E. Shelp and Ronald H. Sunderland

THIS VOLUME EXAMINES ONE OF THE "THREE OFFICES" OF Christ for its meaning and relevance for contemporary pastoral ministry. Theologians have used the titles of prophet, priest, and king to explain the person and work of Jesus. Although these characterizations or titles have given some order to our understanding, they do not fully or adequately express what God has done and is doing in Christ.[1] A much more developed and comprehensive Christology is required to achieve this end.[2] Analogously, attempts to restrict a definition or description of Christian ministry to its prophetic,[3] priestly, and servant (kingly)[4] forms are informative but incomplete. Nevertheless, it is reasonable to examine the prophetic, priestly, and servant work of Jesus in order to discern their implications for the continuation of Jesus' ministry in and through the Body of Christ.

The focus here is on priesthood, the role of priest, the person of a priest, and priestly ministries with reference to pastoral ministries of ordained and lay people. One purpose for these explorations is to become better informed about the biblical, theological, and historical resources that may

Earl E. Shelp, Ph.D., is research fellow, Institute of Religion, and assistant professor of medical ethics, Baylor College of Medicine, Houston.

Ronald H. Sunderland, Ed.D., is research fellow, Institute of Religion, Houston.

ground, guide, and correct the ministry of the church today. Pastoral ministry in all its forms does not necessarily need to be bound to or limited by these precedents in practice and thought. Neither does pastoral ministry in all its forms necessarily need to be freed from them. Rather, these precedents warrant study in order to determine where previous understandings ought to be revised and where current practices and doctrines should be modified. One objective for this sort of conversation between academicians and practitioners, past and present, is the practice of a theologically valid and effective pastoral ministry.

As the contributors to this volume demonstrate, priesthood and priestly ministry are particularly appropriate subjects for this sort of critical discussion, primarily because of the difficulty in explaining why Jesus' sufficient priestly ministry should be duplicated or emulated. John Calvin described Christ as priest as the "perpetual intercessor" who "now bears the priestly role, not only to render the Father favorable and propitious to us by an eternal law of reconciliation, but also to receive us as his companions in this great office."[5] If this is true, no further mediatorial act by another individual would be indicated. The priestly office and priestly ministry that are so firmly entrenched in the life of the church, accordingly, seem, on the surface, to be unnecessary and perhaps improper. This conclusion gains force when it is understood that the use of the term priest and the practices of a priest in church history are not clearly precedented in the New Testament era churches. Yet, given the emphasis on sacrifice, worship, and service that mark Christian mission and identity, the development of the office of "priest" and "priestly acts" representing the person and work of Jesus probably was inevitable.[6]

This evolution within the church of a priesthood appears biblically and theologically valid when the affirmation in 1 Peter (2:9) is heard: "But you are a chosen race, a royal priesthood, a holy nation, God's own people, that you may declare the wonderful deeds of him who called you out of darkness into his marvelous light. Once you were no people but now you are God's people; once you had not received mercy but now you have received mercy." Lesslie Newbigin interprets this verse to mean that the whole church as the Body of Christ is where the love of God is made available to people, where forgiveness is mediated. "The truth is that it is only because the one priestly body has been given from the beginning a structure which includes a ministry based on and continuous with the ministry of the incarnate Lord Himself, that there is a priestly character in the ministry answering to the priestly character of the body. And the supreme function of the priestly ministry is so to minister that the whole body attains to and retains its true priestly character."[7] The task for the priestly people and its representatives in the office of priest is to identify with and participate in the priestly ministry of the Lord. Priestly service, therefore, occurs in free and continuous bidirectional expressions of love. According to Newbigin, these offerings are "like the woman who broke into the Pharisee's house and annointed the feet of Jesus with her tears and her ointment, not because there is any rule to that effect, but because love brims over."[8]

Even though certain biblical texts can be cited as explicit or implicit warrants for a perpetual Christian priesthood, questions remain and, among churches, differing understandings and practices persist. For example, is priesthood a designation for the whole church, or for selected individuals within the church, or both? What is the source of priestly authority, and how is this authority properly exercised? What is the appropriate manner of selecting priests? What are the criteria for and significance of ordination? How is ministerial authority transmitted from generation to generation? These questions and other relevant issues regarding the priestly task of pastoral ministry are addressed by the contributors to this volume.

J. Robert Nelson initiates the examination of priestly ministry by discussing theological and ecclesiastical issues. He observes that churches have developed patterns of ministry, applied biblical names to them, and thereby justified them. These "creative" uses of scripture are questionable, according to Nelson. One does not need to be "creative," however, to demonstrate biblically the priesthood of all believers or of the whole body of Christ. Priestly succession, according to this view, is in the whole body of Christ's people, ordained and unordained, who bear the primary priestly role. If this is so, he asks, how does one legitimate and understand ordained ministry? An answer to this inquiry is developed by examining three conditions in which ordained ministry can be in harmony with the example of ministry in the New Testament. Nelson notes that recent ecumenical investigations reflect an emerging agreement that the authority for ordained ministry is a gift to be exercised in the continuing edification of the Body of Christ, principally through the eucharist at which an ordained person presides as a representative priest of the priestly people. The same representative function attends the rite of baptism. Even as this view gains acceptance across denominational lines, Nelson observes, in concluding, that the debate among the churches about ordained ministry has been focused and continues to focus on ministry as function or character, doing and being.

Gerald Moede traces the evolution of priesthood in the church, noting, in the process, certain difficulties associated with attempts to be both priestly and pastoral at the same time. Moede's historical review of Christian priesthood encompasses the New Testament witness, the experience within the early church and into the Middle Ages. He explains why the term priest was variously applied to certain individuals in Jewish scripture, Jesus, the entire people of God, and a cultic functionary with a special possession of the Holy Spirit, particularly within Roman Catholicism.

Against this experience that tended to separate the priest from the people, Moede contrasts John Wesley's emphasis on preaching at the expense, perhaps, of the corporate expression of the church and its worship in the Lord's Supper. Either emphasis in isolation from the other, according to Moede, can lead to an understanding of ministry that is one-sided and unbalanced. As a guard against a too individualistic view of priesthood and the aberrations associated with it, he urges a return to the early Christian corporate understanding and exercise of ministry. The proper focus in such ministry is on Christ and on the centrality of the church in which the Spirit acts. The priest and preacher serve in relation to, not in isolation from, the apostolic community. The priest in this type of Christian community is one who incarnates the spirit of the church and is publicly consecrated to the service of the gospel. In short, he or she is a public reminder that all Christians belong to God and live in vital relation to the Body of Christ in and through which the Holy Spirit acts.

Dale Moody extends Moede's biblical study of priesthood but focuses on the apostle Paul's understanding of his priestly role and service. Moody defines priest as a person, or people, held to have special access to God on behalf of another person or people. The authority of this role results, according to Moody, from being an object of God's choice, an authority that penetrates the being of the person or group, not just the role or function. He explains that Paul's priestly authority was apostolic, based primarily on Paul's experience and expertise. The nature and forms of this authority are revealed in Paul's apostolic message, ministry, and mission, which Moody describes. He proposes, in concluding, that Paul's priestly authority, grounded in his experience with the risen and living Lord Jesus, become a model for all priestly authority. This form of authority has an eternal validity not tied to ordination, and available in Paul's time and now. As Moody sees it, the issue in the postbiblical era regarding the transfer of priestly authority is the validity either of the theory of apostolic succession or of the claim of direct access to God through some special relation.

George Tavard considers another priestly image in scripture, asking what, if any, implications or interpretations it may have for contemporary ministry. The priestly image is that of Melchizedek. Tavard reviews and analyzes understandings of Melchizedek in Jewish scripture, the Letter to the Hebrews, writings by selected Church Fathers, John Calvin, and contemporary ecumenical thought. These probings turn on the question of the meaning Melchizedek may have for ministry today. Tavard proposes that the image of Melchizedek points to the high priest who calls others to participate in his offering of bread and wine. Accordingly, this image is said by Tavard to have several implications for modern ministry. (a) The symbol of the high priesthood of the risen Lord provides ministers with a point of reference for self-understanding and continuing spiritual formation. Christ is the mediator; ministers are his messengers. (b) The image of Melchizedek should help ministers and congregations to recover a deeper sense of the importance of religious symbols. (c) The image can help modern piety and devotion to pass from Jesusology to an authentic Christology that stresses the universal elements in the saving function of Christ. And (d), the image may help restore Christian liturgy to its rightful place and proper structure.

Constance Parvey, continuing the discussion of priestly authority, broadens the examination of the practice of ordination that was begun by Nelson in the opening chapter. She admits that important questions regarding priestly ministry and priesthood are multifaceted and inseparable from considerations of ecclesiology. She addresses these complex issues regarding priesthood and ordination under rubrics of "why," "who," and "for what." Her analysis of these matters constitutes a feminist critique and response to the World Council of Churches document *Baptism, Eucharist, and Ministry* (BEM). Parvey explains that the model of ministry for women is the New Testament portrayal of Jesus, whose ministry was characterized by healing, mission, outreach, education, and reconciliation. The feminist emphasis regarding ministry is not based on Christ as Lord of the church, with the ordained minister as Christ's representative to the people. She grants that ordained ministers have a representative role, but she argues that they represent the whole people and the whole apostolic tradition, which includes women. The locus of authority, for Parvey, is more properly found in community or from below, rather than being hierarchical and patriarchal. She implies that ordination commissions a person to a bidirectional representative function and responds to an authority that is both gift and responsibility. Her view of ordination that accents notions of wholeness and inclusiveness challenges churches to validate calls and gifts of women and others who heretofore have been excluded because they did not fit a preconceived and questionably valid norm. Further, she argues, against traditional hierarchical understandings, that the purpose of ordination is to empower persons to represent and oversee tasks entrusted to them by the community that embodies the mission of the church. The whole church and its mission, according to the author, are empowered by the Holy Spirit, including the church's representatives who proclaim and serve. Parvey concludes with the suggestion that a more vital pneumatology in the church, as well as a revised ecclesiology, would correct and enrich contemporary understandings and practices of ordination.

The volume ends with an essay by William Willimon that emphasizes the basis and object of ministry in "community." Willimon claims, on the basis of Ephesians 4:4–6, that the gift of the Holy Spirit in baptism is the basis for the creation of Christian community. Further, he claims that unity within community is a condition for the Christian mission to be realized. Willimon notes, however, that achieving and maintaining unity in the Pauline churches was a problem, and remains a problem in churches today. Because of the critical role of community in the Christian mission, Willimon argues that creating community was a task of pastors and teachers during the era of the New Testament, and he speculates that community is *the* reason for the creation of ordained ministry within the church. As a representative person, an ordained individual (priest) has a crucial role in holding a diverse people known as Christians in a unified, functioning, faithful body. This task is facilitated by an understanding of what Willimon characterizes as internal or theological requisites for unity in a congregation. Further, he explores how unity may be achieved through priestly activities, including rites of initiation and of intensification in the worship of God. In the contemporary church, Willimon thinks that the pastor symbolizes the life and identity of a particular congregation and of the universal church. The priestly office and function is legitimate principally in its ability to awaken the baptismally bestowed ministries of all Christians. Even though such an emphasis on the representative priestly office of pastor runs the risk, in practice, of a church becoming a personality cult, Willimon believes that the risk is less if the theological requisites he cites are the basis for a congregation's identity and unity rather than the pastor. In short and in conclusion, Willimon holds that the priest is, above all, a community person, not a super apostle.

Four general themes emerge from these analyses of priesthood and priestly ministry: (1) There are implicit and explicit calls to return to the New Testament for guidance and correction regarding understandings of priesthood and priestly service. Distortions and misunderstandings of the biblical witness over time are seen to have led to aberrations within Roman Catholicism and Protestantism. (2) The authority for priestly ministry is derived from below (community) and from above (Holy Spirit). Maintaining this bidirectional foundation and orientation appears to the contributors to be one way to guard against the excesses and deficiencies associated with concentrating on proclamation or sacraments alone. (3) In addition to the sufficient priesthood of the Christ, the authors emphasize the priestly identity and responsibilities of the whole body of Christ. The ordained person's role is that of a representative priest of a priestly people. And (4), a primary object of concern in priestly ministry is the creation and perpetuation of a unified community. The community's unity, identity, and mission are of crucial importance to the priestly service of the whole body of priests and its representative priests. Through the specific rites or functions presided over by a "community person" (priest), the whole community participates.

These explorations into the priestly office and priestly ministries remind us that priesthood involves responsibility more than privilege. James Wharton's comments regarding the priesthood of Israel are instructive in this regard:

> One does not gain the impression from the Hebrew scriptures that the priest was either dearer to God than other people or had achieved religious "superiority" over any man, woman, or child in Israel. On the contrary, the priest is also totally vulnerable to all the people on whose behalf he ministers. To put it colloquially, the priest is always "on the spot" before God on behalf of the people, and "on the spot" before Israel on behalf of God. . . . It is precisely through living out this "double vulnerability" before God and people that the ministry of priesthood gets its basic biblical character.[9]

This "double vulnerability" of Israel as a nation of priests surely applies to the whole Christian church as a royal priesthood, if the collective arguments of the contributors to this volume are correct. Priestly service, accordingly, becomes representative of and participates in a more comprehensive Godly task of reconciliation.

CHAPTER 1

The Ministry as Function and Being

J. Robert Nelson

Ministry in a Sense Not So Common

THERE IS NO COMMONSENSE REASON WHY CHRISTIAN PAS-
tors should be considered prophets, servants, or priests simply because long ago Jesus assumed those roles. Indeed, as
judged by common sense, it is presumptuous for pastors to
claim for themselves the offices of Jesus. Beware of the pastor
or preacher whose pretension allows him to say, "I am a
prophet." As for being a servant, let him or her be judged by
actions, not by claims. And if the Letter to the Hebrews can
be understood rightly, the priestly work of Jesus took place
"once for all" (7:27; 9:26) as the redemptive sacrifice that put
an end to the sacrificial, priestly cult.[1]

Common sense, however sensible, has never• been the
equivalent of Christian faith, much less of theology. The near-
est it has come to these is found in the practice of imitation.

J. Robert Nelson, D.theol., is director, Institute of Religion, Texas Medi-
cal Center, Houston; adjunct professor, department of medicine, Baylor
College of Medicine; and adjunct professor of religion and health care,
University of Texas Health Science Center, Houston.

1

All Christians can attempt to follow the hard pattern of *imitatio Christi*. By strong will and undeviating discipline they can follow "in his steps" (1 Peter 2:21). They can try to cope with every situation or decision by inwardly answering the silent question: What would Jesus do? Because common sense tells us that imitation is the highest compliment, we might even equate this devout and difficult discipline of emulation with true faith. An ordained minister, especially, can thus tread the path of imitation of the Galilean Master in his roles as prophet, self-giving priest, and humble servant. So can a man or woman who is a minister in the broad sense of the servanthood and priesthood of all believers.

It is entirely commendable to commit oneself to following the ideal way of life exemplified by Jesus Christ. This impulse, however, does not constitute a satisfactory basis for a *theological* understanding of the ministry. Without the desire to follow him by imitation, there can be neither true ministry nor discipleship. To some degree, for every person, the *imitatio Christi* is indispensable to one's being a Christian. Yet something more is needed to define a *doctrine* of ministry beyond the general *practice* of it.

This needed factor is the recognition of the continuing, effectual presence of the risen Christ in the church. His presence is effectual in that he continues to exercise his ministry by the operation of the Holy Spirit. The instruments of Christ's continuing ministry are just the persons of faith, the members of the church in all times and places. The total ministry of the church is thus not constituted by our allegiance to Christ; it is constituted by his working in and through us.

This is an affirmation of belief. It transcends the commonsense idea of religious devotees following their teacher, master, or leader. The ministry of Jesus as described in the New Testament certainly remains the pattern of our service, but the real nature of our ministry is determined by the living Christ's action by the Holy Spirit. The characteristics of a

2

prophetic, serving, and priestly ministry as exercised today have meaning because they embody and express the shape and character of Christ's ministry in the first century and for all history.

This affirmation of the priority and perduring effectiveness of Jesus Christ's ministry has become a virtual consensus, shared by theologians of many traditions and communions. It is expressed in a large number of official statements and doctrinal pronouncements of denominational and ecumenical bodies.[2] Even so, it is not to be assumed that the generality of Christians have as yet elevated their thoughts on ministry above the level of commonsense imitation.

This insight about Christ's continuing ministry illuminates many aspects of the church's life. Here only the aspect of priesthood or priestly ministry is kept in focus.

Christ's Priestly Ministry and Ours

A concise expression of the ecumenical consensus was issued by the Fourth World Conference on Faith and Order, held at Montreal in 1963:

> Christ is High Priest; His Church is called to be the true priesthood in the world, holding out to all men the gift of the reconciliation which He has purchased, and offering up on behalf of all men both the sacrifice of praise, thanksgiving and obedience, and the prayer of penitence and intercession. That it may truly be so, the ministers are set for the priestly service of the Gospel in the midst of the priestly people.[3]

Notice that the word priest is used in three senses or dimensions. Jesus Christ is the Priest for all humanity; the church is intended to be a community of priests (or "royal priesthood"); and representative church members are given the special ministry of priestly service.

How does this triple form of the third office of the *munus triplex* fit in our usual vocabulary? Not so well.[4]

3

The word priest can arouse a variety of mental associations and emotional responses. When we hear the word baker, grocer, tailor, or doctor, our mental and emotional responses are probably determined by the connotations of the word that relate to particular bakers or grocers or tailors or doctors we have known. But if we have an affinity or commitment to any religious tradition, we are most likely to be aroused either positively or negatively just by the sound of the word priest. This is true especially for a Christian of any sort. Then our reactions will not be determined so much by particular priests we have known as by our conditioned attitude to the whole class of priests and the general category of priesthood. Obvious differences exist among the attitudes of Roman Catholics, Anglicans, Presbyterians, and Baptists. So great are these differences of association and response that our very effort to discuss calmly "the priestly role" is called into question. Even if one is not a Christian, or even a religious believer, but a deliberate or de facto nonbeliever, he or she is unlikely to hold a neutral, dispassionate view of priesthood.

Why do we have such strong and contrary feelings about priests and priesthood? Not so much because of deliberate, reasoned choice as because of influential and prejudicial pedagogy of hundreds of years of the several historical traditions in which we stand. To explain and justify the last statement would require an extended retelling of our churchly histories; but it is not so susceptible to being challenged as to require such defense. If the effect of the weight of history is virtually self-evident in this matter of priesthood, then why do we bother to emphasize it? We do so in order to remind ourselves of the need to make a conscious effort to enter the discussion with open-minded objectivity and disciplined feelings, however difficult that may be.

Priests have been distinctly significant persons in all sorts of human societies since unremembered eras. In essence, they have been the ones who perform ritual acts and thereby dispense the graces, promises, assurances, and powers of

4

healing, cleansing, good fortune, divination, and salvation.[5] It is assumed that they have a distinct relation to supernatural powers and divinities, and that they play a mediatorial role between the gods and the people of a community. This sacred connection distinguishes the priest from the religious prophet, preacher, teacher, guru, or administrator of religious affairs. All the more does it differentiate the priest from the whole religious or social community. Just as the priest stands *out* from the community, he or she also stands *for* the community and even *over against* it as the agent of divinity.

Another feature of priesthood that separates it in some cultures from other religious ministries is its hereditary character. Although it *may* be true that the son of an Eastern Orthodox or Anglican priest may become one, it is *only* in virtue of sonship that an ancient Jew of the Levites could be a priest, or a Hindu then and now of the Brahmin caste. This genetic and genealogical factor makes the uniqueness of the priest all the more emphatic.

One other phenomenological aspect should be noted. It is the outward appearance, with its robe or badge of priestly office. The Buddhist's shaven head and yellow robe, the Brahmin's sacred thread, the Russian Orthodox beard, the Roman collar, and, of course, the vestments, rings, crowns, pectoral crosses, and episcopal croziers—whatever the source and meaning of their symbolism, they clearly set priests apart from ordinary folk and, until recently, from most American Protestant preachers.

The qualifying phrase "until recently" is important. How can one account for the blossoming of embroidered robes, stoles, paraments, rainbow stocks, and crosses all over the ecclesial landscape? Is it only a change of popular taste, as with clothing fashions? Does it show a faltering of Protestant puritanism with respect to worship? Or, may it not signal the return to an archetypal, long-suppressed intuition: that being a minister ordained to the gospel and the sacraments implies not only a priestly function, but also a priestly identity? If this be the case, then it presents a danger, the consequences of which are already evident. The danger is the deceptive temptation to think that dressing up in vestments to look like a priest is a sufficient change or improvement of ministerial service, without, at the same time, achieving integrity in sacramental and liturgical theology. Fortunately, there are growing numbers today who understand that a clarified liturgical theology should precede the adoption of ecclesiastical vesture. Clothes may seem to make the successful man or woman, but not the priestly minister.

Neither does the adoption of the name priest make one. Here we run the risk of confusion in trying to rehabilitate that concept and name in Protestant Christianity. The problem is partly one of semantics and etymology.

The English word priest is a shortening of "presbyter," which in turn is a transliteration of the Greek word for elder, *presbuteros*. This seems a good enough argument for some people to assume that priest, presbyter, and elder are three words for the same ministerial office. This assumption is contradicted by the actual practice of differing communions in designating their ministers. A Roman Catholic priest may properly be called a presbyter; a Methodist elder may also justly be called a presbyter. But this nomenclature does not make the Catholic and Methodist to be alike. Names equal to the same name are not equal to each other.

Regrettably the New Testament language does not resolve the problem of discrepancies. In fact, it complicates the problem. As frequently emphasized,[6] the New Testament identifies no priest of the church in the sense that history has given the office. Most scholars agree that the Greek *hiereus* applies to only three kinds of person: the Jewish priesthood or high priest (Mark 1:44; Luke 10:31, John 11:49); Jesus Christ as the Son of God who sacrifices himself in atonement for sin (Hebrews 6:20); and the royal priesthood, which is the whole membership of the church (1 Peter 2:9; Revelation 1:6). By the second century the office of sacrificing priest was being defined and accepted as comparable to the ancient Jewish priesthood and the *sacerdos* of pagan Roman religion.[7] Scholars speak of the "dark tunnel" that connects the New Testament community with the developing threefold ministry of deacon, presbyter/priest, and bishop of the second century. Lacking information and knowledge of that century of transition, it has been easy for churches to assert the identity of *their own* forms or orders of ministry with those of the New Testament. This presumes the apostolic warrant and nature of their ministries. And because the words or names are biblical, the presumption is all the more credible: *diakonos, presbuteros, episkopos*. This reading *back* into the New Testament in such a way as to appear to be reading *from* it has been practiced as much by Presbyterians, Baptists, and Disciples of Christ as by Roman Catholics, Anglicans, and others.

There is now a virtual consensus among critical biblical scholars that definitive descriptions of New Testament offices of ministry are not to be found in the text. John McKenzie, a noted Catholic scholar, writes:

> He [a Catholic] will not find the title priest used in the New Testament; and if he thinks of the New Testament titles of bishop and deacon as he knows these titles, he misunderstands the New Testament. In fact we do not know the function of those men who appear in the New Testament as bishops [overseers], presbyters [elders] and deacons.[8]

This judgment of recent biblical scholarship comes as unwelcome, unsettling, and even unacceptable news to many Christians. If the Bible is authoritative, then *our* forms and offices of ministry must be found in it. If such definitive authority and description for *our* ministries cannot be derived explicitly from the New Testament, then logically we are driven to one of two positions.

Either it does not matter what kind of ministry we have, or whether we have any. Thus Luther and the original Lutherans were indifferent to particular orders and forms of ministry, and the Quakers decided to do without any orders and forms of ministry. But Luther never could become a Quaker. He believed that God wills the church to have pastoral ministers of the word and the sacraments. In good, earthy language, and with scorn, he wrote in the preface to his *Larger Cate-chism:* "Indeed, even among the nobility there are some louts and skinflints who declare that we can do without pastors and preachers from now on because we have everything in books and can learn it all by ourselves. So they blithely let parishes fall into decay."[9] Luther could not tolerate "spiritualists" who claimed to have immediate revelation and direction apart from Christ, the gospel, and the sacraments. He rejected the radical Thomas Munzer with the memorable, sarcastic charge that "he had swallowed the Holy Ghost, feathers and all."[10]

Or the churches can develop their patterns of ministry, using biblical names, and then justify these patterns, after the fact, by reference to biblical prefigurations of them. By doing it this way Protestants have tacitly admitted something like the Roman Catholic concept of development of doctrine in the stream of Tradition. By this method Catholicism has claimed that bishops continue the role of the original apostles, with the Bishop of Rome standing in unique succession to St. Peter. Likewise, Methodist bishops can claim to be both *presbuteroi* and *episkopoi* in the New Testament sense; and deacons are called successors of St. Stephen. In other words, as honest confrontation and responsible ecumenical dialogue have recently taught us, virtually all churches have accepted the development of Tradition and traditions.[11] The various traditions have hardened over centuries. But today, using the solvent of emerging consensus on biblical interpretation, we can soften those traditions and expect increasing degrees of mutual agreement and recognition.

Priesthood in Christian churches, in particular the sense of the sacrificing, mediating *sacerdos*, likewise requires the theory of doctrinal development to be justified. However, priesthood in the general sense of all believers does not require traditional development. It has been present from the first generation of apostles. This is where the New Testament made a startling break from the common and conventional ideas of priesthood in the ancient religions. The priests are not a special class, a holy order, either by genealogy or by anointing. In early Christianity not only are priestly-type leaders of the church included in the whole community, but also the people as a whole *are* the priesthood when they act together in worship, service, and witness. The great doctrine of the "priesthood of all believers" was not invented by Martin Luther in order to start a reformation of the Western church. The doctrine was already there in Catholicism,[12] but it was covered over and rendered impotent by the papal and hierarchical power. When Luther uncovered it and made it his chief instrument of reform, however, he did not call it "the priesthood of *each* believer." This individualistic construct became rampant and popular after the eighteenth-century Enlightenment of reason and the nineteenth-century individualism. Yet it again concealed and distorted the biblical meaning of the church as "royal priesthood" or "a kingdom of priests." Far from being a biblical basis for personal piety and individual salvation, the priesthood of all the faithful who are baptized into the community of the Body of Christ is the primary human reality of the church. This corporate priesthood is the *human* reality; but the truly primary reality of the church is the person and priestly ministry of the risen Jesus Christ himself. When we ask about, discuss, or debate the historical succession of the church's ministry, the factors of ordained office must come second. The primary succession is the whole body of Christ's people. As a visible social body they constitute the continuing Body of Christ.

Again we encounter some semantical confusion here, just as in saying that Christ as priest constitutes a priestly people. Here the key word is body. Karl Barth was right when he declared that there are not three bodies of Christ, but one. Yet it is seen in three ways: as the body of the incarnate Word of

9

God who lived and died, as the risen body gathering people into the community that makes Christ present in the world, and in the symbolic, eucharistic bread.[13] Therefore, in reference to baptism, which initiates members, and Holy Communion, which sustains them, the whole people as Christ's corporate community have the primary priestly role.

In one of the many hymns written for Methodists to sing during the Lord's Supper, John and Charles Wesley wrote these significant lines: "Ye royal priests of Jesus rise/And join the morning sacrifice."[14] *Who* makes the sacramental sacrifice? *All* the people present, led by their chosen priestly minister.

Where is the Body of Christ to be seen? Wherein is the real presence of the Lord found? In the bread, yes; but more so in the men and women and children who convene to consume it and drink the wine, making their sacrificial gifts of praise and thanksgiving and their expressions of faith and love (Romans 12:1). With more theological sense than sentimentality, one can look on the communicants in the pews or at the altar and hear Jesus say, "These are my body." As the apostle Paul wrote to that contentious, fragmented congregation of Corinth: "Now you *are* the body of Christ and individually members of it [1 Cor. 12:27]." The wide differences of human characteristics and personalities made no difference to Paul in insisting on the unity and community of members of the Body of Christ. The diverse talents and gifts (charismata) of service, ministry, teaching, and mission gave to each member a particular role in the upbuilding of the church in love (1 Corinthians 14:5). Once more: the priesthood, or priestly ministry, of all members is not a proposition derived from an individual's experience of faith, but the essential activity of the community of faith.

This biblical, Pauline assertion about the core reality of the church as the priesthood of the whole body may be seen in three ways. During the history of all churches and in honest

10

consideration of most of them today, the assertion expresses three possibilities.

- It is sheer hyperbole: an exaggerated and utterly unattainable kind of community, suitable perhaps for the best kind of angels but not for human beings like us.
- It is an insidious occasion for hypocrisy because, as an admirable theological doctrine, it tempts church members to pretend they are a loving, serving community when in fact they are not.
- Or, the priesthood of the whole people of a congregation or church assembly, unordained and ordained alike, is the most potent and compelling belief about the ministry that can be confessed.

Without any illusions, the third possible interpretation is commended as the condition to be sought, despite all the familiar debilities of a congregation and the persons who constitute it. Even persons who are uncomfortable with the word priest can welcome the idea of the church as the priestly community, offering their lives to God in faithful obedience, loving service, and worship after the manner of Christ.

The Enigma of Ordination

If the priesthood of all believers is so well established, how can we resolve the perennial, nagging question of the legitimacy and character of the *ordained* ministry? The rules and patterns of ministry in the New Testament are so indeterminate and uncertain that it is hard to refute on biblical grounds *only* the conviction that an ordained ministry is not required. Granted. So, as I have said, the seat of authority for ministry has been widened since the second century to include a tradition that is neither incongruent with the scriptures nor "repugnant" to them—as the Anglican Articles of Religion put it. Is ordination to a special or representative ministry incongruent with the apostolic era's church? Not really. Is the

11

Christian priesthood, which developed later, out of harmony with the New Testament? Yes and no, depending on the theory, concept, and exercise of such priesthood.

Harmony prevails between the Bible and a ministerial priesthood under certain conditions. There are at least three of these.

- First, that the ministry is seen and believed to be derived from, and intentionally continuing, the redemptive ministry of Jesus Christ by the power of the Holy Spirit.
- Second, that the faithful ministry of *all* the people of God who bear Christ's name in baptism is the general expression of the presence of the Body of Christ in the world. The whole body of members takes precedence over and authorizes the special, representative ordained ministries.
- Third, that the ordained ministries are distinctly and definitely determined by the preaching of the gospel, or Word of God, and the administering of the sacraments. These primary services are authorized by the congregation, as representing the church at large, by ordination or consecration, in recognition of the person's calling by the Holy Spirit. It is "an authentic call heard with good conscience," as Presbyterians describe it.

The emerging ecumenical agreement on these conditions is clearly evident in both the *Consultation on Church Union Consensus* and the broader statement of the World Council of Churches' *Baptism, Eucharist, and Ministry*. No documents are more widely representative.

Since ordination is essentially a setting apart with prayer for the gift of the Holy Spirit, the authority of the ordained ministry is not to be understood as the *possession* of the ordained person, but as a gift for the continuing edification of the body in and for which the minister has been ordained.[15]

It is especially in the eucharistic celebration that the ordained ministry is the visible focus of the deep and all embracing communion between Christ and the members of his body.[16]

These two quotations were written and approved by approximately three hundred men and women. They were officially appointed by their denominations or communions, being Eastern Orthodox, Roman Catholic, and most varieties of Protestantism. Yet it would be dishonest or unrealistic to claim that these persons, mostly theologians of good repute, speak for all their constituent memberships. Two questions are suggested by the quotations on which strong differences remain. One is that of the authority of ministry or priestly service as a gift to and possession of the ordained person. The other is the minister's primary focus on the sacrament of Holy Communion. Consider these in sequence.

Is the ministry *only* a function? Or is it also a matter of personal being and identity? Here are two unreconciled concepts or doctrines of ministry and priesthood. It is not accurate to say that all Protestants regard ministry only in functional terms; but it *is* true that Catholics and Orthodox perceive their priests to have a special status or indelible character. That the latter view has an ancient, long-standing history cannot be denied. As Bernard Cooke writes: "While 'ministry' is essentially a functional reality—'priesthood' resists such classification. It is more a state of being, a level of existence, an intrinsic qualification."[17]

In place of presenting the familiar pros and cons of this debate, the distinctions between ministry as being and function can be illustrated by anecdotes. Yet these will not resolve the problem.

Long ago in New York, in a discussion at Union Theological Seminary with theologian Paul Tillich and philosopher Paul Weiss, W. H. Auden of poetic fame made a statement that at first was cryptic and then illuminating. "There are only two pure occupations," said the Anglo-Catholic poet. "Manual labor and the priesthood. The only important question about the laborer is whether he is employed. If not, he is not really a laborer. The only critical question about a priest is this: Is he rightly ordained? If not, he is not a priest."

At Lund, Sweden, in 1952 the Bishop of Durham, Dr. Michael Ramsey, made a deliberately abrasive statement to an ecumenical audience. He intended only to prove his point on priesthood. "If you want to know whether I am a priest of the Church of God," he said, wagging his abundant eyebrows and it seemed almost winking sardonically, "do not analyze my sermons for orthodox doctrine. Do not judge my performance of churchly duties nor my personal piety. But come to my study, and I will show you the certificate of my ordination in the Church of England." (Or words to that effect.)

Now, Anglicans can be angular at times, although at others most reasonable and lovable. But Auden and Ramsey were simply stating in bold and canonical terms what all kinds of Catholics and Orthodox know: that *being* a minister or priest by the grace of God is more important than *doing* something in and for the church. This is perhaps an ineffable quality. It is theologically expressed, even in Protestantism, by the general rule that ministers are not re-ordained. So-called re-ordination can take place only when the ordaining church refuses to recognize the prior act by another church as valid. As the Vatican still holds officially, but with decreasing certainty, Anglican orders such as those of Archbishop Ramsey remain "absolutely null and utterly void!"[18] So, ordination, like baptism, is once only.

What is this ineffable, indefinable character, however? It is dramatized by contrasting the immediate consequences of ordination as observed in a Methodist Conference and in the apse of St. Peter's basilica in Rome.

A dozen or more women and men are ordained in one ceremony by a Methodist bishop. Parents, family, spouses are present. And after the ritual, what do they do? They hug the new minister in the family, say solemn words of congratulation, or even slap backs and utter ecclesiastical wisecracks in a folksy but sincere manner.

Sixty seminarians of the North American College in Rome are ordained in the vast apse of St. Peter's. They prostrate their bodies on the marble floor and rise to receive the imposition of the bishop's hands. The ordinands' parents have flown over to Rome for this singular event. At the close of the liturgy the new priests come to meet their mothers and fathers. What do the parents do? Hug? Congratulate? Joke? No. They kneel before their son and say, "Father, give me your blessing." And he blesses them.

How can one better illustrate the difference between ministry as function and character? Perhaps this way, with a news notice recently received from Bolivia: "Eugenio Poma will be the first Indian to be elected bishop" by the Methodist Church of Bolivia. "He is also the first layperson to be elected bishop—and will continue to be a layman even after his consecration." After four or eight years Bishop Poma will be required to give up the episcopal office, but his status as a layman will remain unchanged.

Michael Ramsey and Eugenio Poma belong equally to the general priesthood of all believers. But they represent opposite poles of belief and theology about ministry. These extremes cannot be reconciled.

Neither can we be sanguine enough to think that characteristic members of many Protestant denominations will agree with the ecumenical assertion that the ordained ministry is the focal point of communion between Christ and the church, "especially in the eucharistic celebration." According to this understanding, the communion between Christ and the church would occur only as frequently as the eucharist is celebrated. Or not at all in churches that practice lay celebration of the Lord's Supper. So we still have problems.

In one sense the ecumenical convergence is clearly happening. It is bringing the extremes of functionalism and character, doing and being, toward a meeting point. At this nexus, not yet reached, people will see the ordained minister leading a fully participating congregation in the eucharistic celebration, after he or she has proclaimed and interpreted the Word of God and led the prayers of the people. The minister in this priestly function will preside at the eucharist not because he or she is "better at it" than anyone else, or because of possession of a sacred power and persona that puts him or her in a Brahmin-like caste. To the contrary, the minister (by the imposition of hands and the invocation of the Holy Spirit) will accept the authority and the priestly role that have been bestowed by the people of the church as their called and chosen representative.

As representative priest of the priestly people, the minister takes the lead for the congregation in the common celebration of baptism and the Lord's Supper. There are exceptional circumstances, apart from the regular gathering of the people for worship, when the minister's role in the sacraments (or ordinances) may be supplanted by other members of the "royal priesthood." But here we speak of the normal, settled life of the church.

Present theology of ministry and sacraments has fortunately rendered obsolete the most unfortunate aberration of priesthood in the Middle Ages of Europe, that is, when the priest was the *dispenser* of grace to the people, in the same way that a feudal monarch or lord might dispense justice or small favors to an ignorant and unfranchised peasantry. More apt for church practice today is the analogy of minister/priest to a judge rather than to an autocrat. Judges who hear arguments and hand down decisions do not do so merely as mouthpieces of a majority of the citizenry. Nor, even less, do they make rulings out of their own arbitrary thoughts and in virtue of their persons. Judges indeed have a status, an identity that surpasses their functioning. But they judge according to a law that is always higher in authority than their own opinion and confront the citizenry only as its representatives who are appointed to serve society under the higher law.

The minister's priestly role, likewise, has a dual reference. In one sense the minister is the chosen representative of all the people of the church or, in some polities, of the members of a congregation. Priestly and pastoral activities may then be seen as rather ordinary human concerns. In the other sense, by the church's recognizing this person's calling and conferring the status of ordained minister, those same activities have a distinct relation to God's purpose.

Our ways of describing, interpreting, and evaluating the ordained ministry always incur the opposite dangers of trivializing and exalting it. By a commonly expressed reductionism it is asserted that sermons are merely moral discourses, prayers are autosuggestions, sacraments are just archaic rituals, and ordained ministers are employed to perform these functions. The opposite extreme is sacerdotalism, or priestcraft, which has been amply discredited by historical experience and theological discernment. The tension between humiliation and exaltation of the ministry is a sign of the ministry's dependence on Jesus Christ. Still in his divinized humanity and his humanized divinity, Christ provides the analogy for the whole church and the priestly ministry.

CHAPTER 2

Priest and Pastor: Lessons from Our Predecessors

Gerald F. Moede

IN THIS ESSAY I BEGIN WITH AN INVESTIGATION OF THE evolution of the priesthood in the church, noting the difficulty it encountered in exercising a pastoral ministry over the centuries. In a second section I use Methodism as a case study in pointing out that an intentional prophetic ministry met some of the same difficulties in remaining pastorally effective and authentic. In a concluding section I trace elements of new thinking that give us hope of filling in some past gaps in a more fully pastoral ministry that might be both prophetic and priestly in a way congruent to the New Testament's intention of Christian ministry. In an essay of this short scope it is necessary to use generalizations, to which exceptions can readily be found. But I have tried to be both accurate and fair, and I hope constructive, in looking toward effective pastoral ministry for the future.

Gerald F. Moede, D.theol., is general secretary, Consultation on Church Union, and visiting fellow, Princeton Theological Seminary, Princeton, New Jersey.

The Development of Priestly Ministry

Ministry in the Early Days—New Testament

It is well known that in the New Testament the only individuals named priest are those of the Old Testament and Jesus.[1] There is a priesthood of the entire people of God (1 Peter), but never of a leader of worship or oversight. Jesus is seen as high priest and prophet (Hebrews 3:1), even though he was not himself a priest.

In fact, there is no one in the New Testament to whom cultic ministry is officially or exclusively committed; it is difficult to define cult in the New Testament church.[2]

Israel had had priests, as keepers of the temple and leaders of ceremony. Jewish priesthood was a national institution. Priests had authority to offer sacrificial victims on the altar in Jerusalem and conduct other rituals of the temple cultus. Only the priest had a right to occupy the sacred precinct called the Holy Place.[3]

But priests did not intervene on behalf of the people. They did teach Israel the law and the demands of covenant and cared for the daily sacrifice in the temple. But in a real sense, even in the Old Testament, all the people are priests (Exodus 19:4–6; Isaiah 61:6), with a priestly mission to all people. After the development of the synagogue during the exile, the synogogue was presided over by elders; the rabbi was a lay person.

Jesus never commended a priest, as an individual or as an altar functionary. In fact, he used priests as examples of the wrong kind of religion (Luke 10:31–32). All the texts that refer to Jesus' priesthood point to *his self*-offering. Such texts as these can be mentioned: 1 Timothy 2:5–6; Hebrews 10:11–18; Hebrews 9:14 and 10:14. In Hebrews 9:14 Jesus is both priest and victim; he identifies himself with humanity in Hebrews 10:21.

Biblical passages like Revelation 21:22–22:5 glorify a priestly calling. Jesus' servants *are* priests and their ministry is priesthood. "It was the deep impression made by Jesus' life and death as showing a unique obedience and a devotion to God and man, that caused the community to describe Jesus' death in terms of cultic images."[4] In Christ there was a total offering.

So in the New Testament we find no Christian priests. Nor do we find a description of the duty or work of a presbyter. But texts referring to these places of leadership indicate pastoral or teaching rather than hieratic ministry—such as serving in ordination (1 Timothy 4:14) and anointing of the sick (James 5:14). There are scattered references to their ministry, such as general oversight of their churches and guarding from false teachers, preaching and teaching, setting examples of service (Acts 20:17; 1 Timothy 5:17; 1 Peter 5:1–4; Hermas 2:4; 3).[5] Their leadership was seen as *service*, not as governance or ruling or even of presiding (even 2 Corinthians 1:24).

Toward the end of the first century there was a church order according to which a group of "presbyters" was responsible for the leadership and pastoral care of the local communities (Acts 14:23; 20:17, 20–30; 1 Peter 5:1; 1 Timothy 3:1–7). The presbyters were called *episkopoi*, without any perceptible difference—they had the function of oversight.[6]

Finally, in regard to this era, we can say that ministry in the New Testament did not develop from and around the eucharist or liturgy, but from the apostolic building up of the community through preaching, admonition, and leadership.[7] Ministry at this time was intentionally apostolic—first in the sense of the apostolicity of the gospel of the community. Because they are leaders and pioneers, they must in fact be the least in the community. Churches did have presiding officers, but because the synogogue was their model, these persons led in prayer, teaching, and reading, not priestly ministry in the sense of offering sacrifice. We have no idea who presided at the Lord's Supper during this time (in 1 Corinthians 11 Paul left no instructions on that subject).

In short, "the early years seemed a-cultic, there was not an institutionalized ritual. Hebrews deals with sacrifice. But it seems to lead to the conclusion that sacrificial cult is not only unnecessary, but inappropriate in the Christian community— Christian sacrifice has been offered once and for all" (Apostolic Tradition 3).[8] No longer were sacrifices of atonement needed (nothing can or need be added to that of Christ), "but sacrifices of thanks and praise for what Christ has perfected, not sacrifices of external gifts, but the offering of oneself (let us continually offer up a sacrifice of praise to God [Heb. 13:15]."[9]

The Priest in the Early Church

During the second century the presbyter/bishop assumed general presidency of the Lord's Supper.[10] But throughout the subapostolic period there is still a noticeable absence of cultic language in reference to the persons who exercised leadership, even in the Pastoral Letters.

Many writers attribute the "cultifying" of Christianity to a growing influence of the Old Testament in the early church, even though resistance to introducing the restrictions of Old Testament law represented a kind of break with Jewish priesthood. Indeed, some believe that this is why it seemed permissible to introduce a Christian priesthood! As the eucharist became more formal, the idea of *sacerdotium* emerges in Hippolytus. Bishops and presbyters thereby became increasingly cult personnel.[11] Thus by the end of the second century *hiereus* was being used in the Greek-speaking church, and *sacerdos*, in the Latin-speaking parts. And during the same era the presbyter was being overshadowed by the bishop. Early in the second century the person who gave unity to the community presided, with the celebration understood as a concelebration between the community and the priest, who was a servant of all.[12]

In Ignatius of Antioch there was still a certain similarity to the thought of the New Testament. The community life described is paralleled with that of Christ and the disciples. The same is true with Justin. But as early as Clement of Rome the Old Testament pattern of hierarchy was invoked as explanation for the same kind of hierarchical structure in Christianity.[13] Also with Clement arose a distinction between clergy and laity. This was visible in Ignatius as well. But in these writers there was still a basic unity between clergy and lay.

I have noted that the use of "priest" to denote a minister occurs first in Hippolytus, and in that he refers to a bishop. In his prayer of ordination Hippolytus called the bishop "high priest." But there is no word here regarding the liturgical functions of the presbyter, only his care and governance of the church with fellow presbyters and bishop. The New Testament conception of the whole church as priesthood continues into the third century (Justin Martyr, *Dialogue with Trypho*, 116:3; Irenaeus, *Against Heresies*, iv., 8,3; Origen, *Commentaries on John*, 1.2).[14] But already by 200 Tertullian refers to the bishop as *summus sacerdos* (*On Baptism*, 17). There is no hint, however, of any sacerdotal *character* at this time. And it can still be said that the basic pastoral ministry included prophecy, witness, teaching, as well as liturgical leadership and preaching. It was still true, as Cooke so aptly puts it, that the basic pastoral right and responsibility to teach were rooted in the "pastor's" possession of understanding, not in the pastor's occupying an office or status in the community.[15]

But a constant evolution was taking place. *Sacerdotium*, as used by Basil of Alexandria, was the *cultic function* exercised principally by bishops but shared with presbyters—it was the corporate provision for the worship of God through union with Christ's priestly sacrifice.[16] The corporate dimension of this worship was slowly eroding, however. Thus by Nicaea resistance to the term *sacerdos* was pretty well gone, although it was still not the usual term for a presbyter.

Priesthood into the Middle Ages

The period of the Middle Ages was a complex time, when ministerial functions and understandings in the church were undergoing a basic shift. The cultic focus of ministerial responsibility took on more and more importance during this time. Whereas in the early Christian community *episkopos* described better than *hiereus* the function of the ministry (pastorally supervising the life of the community), now cultic aspects of this role began to take precedence and the two terms became interchangeable.[17]

Harsh judgments about this shift were made later in church history, to the effect that the Old Testament categories were creeping back into the church, and thus suppressing the radical newness of the gospel that had characterized the New Testament church. Cooke reminds us that a number of elements in early Christian history seem to be linked to this shift: the decline of prophecy, the lessening interest in ecclesiology, the ethicizing of "the law of Christ," and the emergence of hierocracy.[18] Although we can point out some of these dangers (in retrospect), we can better understand the reasons for the shift as well. "After all, it is hard enough to grasp Old Testament faith and the gospel is yet more challenging, with its message of new life and its faith in 'the Word made flesh.'"[19]

The outward manifestation of basic changes taking place in exercise and conception of ministry was centered in understanding the eucharist, and thus in the ordination of presbyter/priest/bishop. When ordination was understood as placing a person into an order, it gave the person the responsibility to perform certain functions, centering on the eucharist, which required a certain *power*. This power was associated with a special possession of the Spirit, and this appears early in the ordination prayer.

Both Augustine and Chrysostomos were influential in this evolution of thought and practice. The priest was gradually acting ministerially *for* Christ in the sacraments; in this change the laity became further removed from the activity in the Lord's Supper. In this line of thought Christ continues to offer his sacrifice in the supper (Chrysostomos, *In Matt.*, Hom. 50:5). The same point of view can be found in Ambrose. Through Leo I, Gregory I, Isidore of Seville, the doctrine passes into medieval thought.

Cooke describes the evolution clearly:

> In the Middle Ages a subtle shift in pastoral orientation occurred. In early times the priest was acting for the benefit of the present and worshipping community, so they [the community] might become more deeply identified with and embodied in the Church, identified *with* the church and with the mystery of Christ, on which the life of the Church depended. In later stages, there is less of this emphasis and more stress on obtaining the benefits of the sacrifice of Christ for those present, but also for others—living and dead, for whom Mass was offered. . . . [It shifts from] a mystery action to a cause of grace. The ministry of the priest is viewed less as sacrament and more as instrument.[20]

Furthermore, as the role of the priest focuses more on applying the benefits of Christ's passion, the earlier practice of penance moves more toward confession and absolution. When this happens the priest soon becomes an intermediary for Christ.

Such a shift obviously reduced the sense of wholeness of the body and separated those ordained from the lay people. It also gradually brought about the perception that those ordained (especially the bishops) made up a particularly sacred group, that they stood in a closer relationship with God, and that with their special power they could approach the altar in a special way. In this evolution it is also understandable why celibacy begins to grow in strength, first as an expectation and later as a legal necessity.

Thus, whereas ordained ministry early had been ministry of word and sacrament, now priesthood as a cultic leadership gains center stage in preference to apostolic preaching, and the early breadth of pastoral ministry comes to be focused in fewer dimensions. In the early church the Old Testament had influenced the idea of the bishop as *pastor* (shepherd); by the twelfth century the Old Testament foundation of ministry was focused on the Aaronic priesthood.

The Institutionalization of Priesthood

In descriptive fashion I shall note some of the factors that contributed to the hardening of the understanding and practice of priesthood in the church. No attempt will be made to be complete in this bird's-eye view, but the attempt to understand would not be authentic without at least mention of some of these factors.

"Power" More Than "Gift"

I have already indicated the growing use and focus on the idea of sacrifice in the ministry and eucharist of the church which characterized the time from Nicaea until after the Fourth Lateran Council. The authority of the eucharist in the life of the church as the anamnesis of Christ's sacrifice gave to those who presided over it a profound association with Christ's personal sacrificial self-offering.[21]

A second factor in changing the dominant idea regarding the ordained person had to do with "unfaithful" priests who had "fallen away" (and then returned) and those who had lived in a less than holy way during times of persecution. From these stimuli had arisen great debates as to the efficacy of ministry performed by priests in various degrees of sin or schism. Over the years the church had generally decided that the effectiveness of one's ministry did not depend on a certain degree of holiness. And such an approach led almost inevitably to a belief that there was something almost automatic in the power given to this person in ordination that worked in spite of oneself.

But this was an aberration of early church tradition, in which the person ordained was given authority to act as a *word* of the church. In this understanding the effectiveness of one's action would come from that action being the *church's* word, not from some other power that was attached to the office through ordination.

Another factor was this: when presbyterial ordination came to be viewed as the conferring of causal power *(potestas ordinis)*, the sense of collegiality among presbyters and bishops was greatly reduced. In such a situation all priests had their own power individualized, and the relation to other ordained persons, and especially to the laity, was seen to be unnecessary or, at best, unimportant. Out of this view "private masses," with no people assembled, became common. The priest was seen as operating in an individualistic manner, without need of the community. Grace was bought "at a distance" for those for whom the Mass was being offered. Stipends helped to increase this practice.

Edward Schillebeeckx reminds us that it was canon lawyers who developed the "power" concept to its fullness. This development resulted in "absolute ordination"; by virtue of ordination a priest had all priestly power in his own person. "It now became a sacred rite and set a man apart from a particular *ecclesia,* and this opened the way to the private mass. A man now had the 'power of the eucharist.' The consequence was that the old relationship between *ministerium* and *ecclesia* now shifts to a relation between *potestas* and *eucharistia,* the power to consecrate the eucharist."[22]

Another result of this change was that the priesthood came to be seen more as a personal state of life, a *status,* than as a service in and to the community, leading later to the "indelible character" thinking. Whereas ordination had earlier suggested "being directed toward" and helped create a new interrelatedness to a particular eucharistic community, the danger now was that it brought about a "director of," or a "manipulator of," that could be carried out even in the absence of any community.

Eucharist as Change: Validity as Key

A second group of factors to identify during this era includes the increasing mention of the sacerdotal power (referred to earlier) being over the Body of Christ in the eucharist. This has to do with Christ, not primarily with the community.

> The shift is clear; it is now one of changing bread and wine into Christ, and this is the precise concentration of priestly power in the action. And so the disputes begin (in the ninth century), disputes as to whether the bread really becomes Christ; if so, how this can be explained; the eucharistic mode of presence becomes the "real" presence. In such a shift of understanding about the action performed, the agent becomes . . . the worker of wonders, the agent of transubstantiation.[23]

The "character" question of the ordained person also became more complex. Since the time of Augustine the power of the keys, as a social power and authority, had begun to include a sacramental "character," a kind of intrinsic qualitative reality in the priest. This endowed the person in question with the power of transforming the elements in the eucharist by the words of consecration. The basic change involved the presiding person's perceived role as now being instrumental rather than sacramental.

So the main thrust of discussion came to be whether the celebrant of the Lord's Supper was causally effective, and such discussion led to more juridical concerns having to do with "validity." By the twelfth century the view had emerged that the eucharistic celebrant makes Christ present, not by being there himself as sacramental, but by transforming the bread and wine. Thus the basic shift—from the celebrant as the sign of Christ's presence to the consecrated elements as that sign—from mystery action to real presence.[24]

I have now described, in almost outline fashion, an evolution from a more pastoral ministry of the early church to a juridical and instrumental focusing on power and efficacy. It became primarily eucharistic activity to which the priest was ordained; the preaching and community leadership foci went into obscurity. Although theologically it was still God who was acting in transubstantiation, the emphasis was certainly on the priest as acting on the bread and wine by changing them. Any sense of the community of Christians acting sacramentally in the celebration seemed lost, or certainly obscured. The power to confect as eucharistic celebrant and that of the keys, exercised in sacramental absolution, was central. The Council of Trent made this double focus abundantly clear; preaching became preparatory to sacramental activity.

A description in theological terms of what happened is succinctly made by Schillebeeckx:

> The first Christian millennium expressed its view of the ministry chiefly in ecclesial and pneumatological terms, or better, pneumatological-christologically, whereas second millennium gave the ministry a directly christological basis and shifted the mediation of the church into the background. In this way a theology of the ministry developed without an ecclesiology. . . .
>
> The sacrament will later be defined in a technical and abstract sense as *signum efficax gratiae*, in which the ecclesial dimension remains completely unconsidered. Its sacramental power is founded directly on the "sacred" power which is the priest's personal possession. In this way the ecclesial significance of the ministry with its charismatic and pneumatological dimensions is obscured, and the more time goes on, the more the ministry is embedded in a legalistic cadre which bestows sacred power.[25]

Another Roman Catholic theologian, Walter Kasper, puts it this way:

> After the first thousand years or so of the Church's history, interest was no longer centered upon the activity of God made

28

present in the office of the Church. The analytically-minded theologians of the scholastic period were more interested in the inner structure of the sacramental signs, their efficacy and validity. They thus gave more prominence to the task of establishing criteria of validity which could be applied to the Church's office.[26]

Interlude

Christians agree that Christ is the one high priest, and that anything else called priesthood is so because it stands in some special relation to his unique priesthood. But what that means has varied from time to time. Was it a onetime sacrifice that Christ had made? Was it to be repeated? How are its benefits appropriated? Does the church offer sacrifice, or does it "remind God" by repeating an act that has sacrificial dimensions? Or does it plead God's mercy on the basis of Christ's sacrifice?

Behind these questions lie some deep soteriological differences. How is salvation accomplished and offered in Christ? How is it received by believers? What is the relation of the church to the minister/priest? The Council of Trent, where much of this came together in the Roman Catholic Church, said that salvation is mediated in the priestly act of offering sacrifice; offering sacrifice was the most proper action of the ordained minister, in its opinion.[27] A serious breach was developing, since Protestant Reformers were emphasizing the process of faith being aroused by God's Word, and claiming that no further sacrifice was necessary or possible.

Ministry is needed to preserve in a living way the apostolicity of the community's tradition. Giving it specific form needs to be a pastoral as well as a cultic question, which the church needs always to consider again and again.

After noting how the Reformers emphasized the pastoral ministry, I will examine another ecclesial tradition (Methodist) in which the development of ministry moved in a direction almost exactly opposite from that just portrayed. I have noted earlier how the various dimensions of pastoral ministry tended to be weakened in the general preoccupation in the Roman Catholic tradition of the Middle Ages with sacrifice and the person of the ordained in relation to cultic ministry. This weakening also occurred in Methodism for almost the opposite reason.

The Lutheran Reformation kept the "pastor" as the one basic office.[28] Martin Bucer stressed the pastoral dimension as well, along with the activity of the entire community. In John Calvin's polity, pastors were central, with preaching and the administration of the sacraments clearly allied with teaching. Underlying these varieties of emphasis was a deep difference: the administration of the Lord's Supper as a representative ministry was differentiated from a cultic offering of sacrifice as the proper role of the eucharistic celebrant. This difference is only now finding some hope of resolution, as the ministry of the Word and the priesthood of all the Body are again being emphasized in the ecumenical discussion.

I turn now to note a different kind of one-sided development within Methodism.

Preacher/Pastor/Priest in Methodism

John Wesley was ordained a priest in the Church of England in 1728. At the time he could be termed a "high churchman," taking the sacramental life of that church and its rites and practices with the utmost seriousness. At this juncture in his life he returned from helping his father as a curate in a parish to the life of a fellow at Oxford, where he began to minister to the sick, the needy, and the prisoners in and around that city. The seemingly rigid and ascetic life led by Wesley and his colleagues earned them the nickname "Methodists." But here was an attempt at a balanced pastoral ministry that combined regular participation in the eucharist with other pastoral dimensions, such as comforting the sick, feeding the hungry, visiting those in prison, counseling the perplexed, holding

services of prayer and renewal, and instructing those interested in Christian moral guidelines.

When Wesley began preaching outdoors a decade later,
most parish churches were closed to him. His passion was to
spread the good news around the country, counseling people
to "flee from the wrath to come,"urging them to live lives of
scriptural holiness. From those who heard him, societies and
classes were assembled; these groups began what came to be,
over the entire British Isles, the Methodist movement.

Wesley intended his to be a movement of renewal *within*
the national church, the "best constituted national church" in
the world, in his opinion. He urged society members to
receive the Lord's Supper at their parish church and participate in the life of the parish. He intentionally avoided planning or holding his own services as to compete with those of
the Church of England, at least in his early years.

The men (and at that point they *were* men!) who made up
this preaching fraternity began to build and travel circuits of
these societies. Their numbers expanded rapidly, until, when
Wesley died in 1791, more than 500 preachers were involved.
For most of his life Wesley insisted this was a supplemental
renewal movement in the Church of England, and therefore
refused to compete.

But as relations with the national church continued to dete-
riorate during the "middle years," this point became more
and more difficult to maintain honestly. This meant that min-
istrations of local Church of England clergy became more
difficult to secure and cooperation from individuals of that
church became more uncommon.

Trying to maintain his view that his people needed to receive the eucharist with regularity (as he did; he partook every
three or four days for most of his ministry), he applied to
various places for ordination for some of his preachers. The
bishop of London refused to ordain any of his men, but a
wandering Orthodox bishop did ordain one of his preachers, a
certain John Jones. This unusual event illustrates the lengths

to which Wesley was prepared to go to secure a "complete" ministry.

And yet he continued to insist at the same time that, although both an inner and an outer call to ministry are desirable, if forced to choose between the two, he would choose the inner as being essential.[29] And in his eyes his preachers had this inner divine call and gifting, even if the national church refused to provide the outer confirmation by ordaining them.

The dichotomy between word and sacrament that this position brought about is one of the original and continuing incongruities of Methodism. One can understand the historical reasons for it in the circumstances of Wesleyan England, where priestly ministry was taking place in the parish churches but conversion, rich and vital faith, and "Christian assurance" were not ordinarily emphasized.

When Wesley's movement spread to the colonies, it was first of all the result of lay peoples' activity. And when Wesley began sending official preachers in 1766, even those men were not ordained. Thus from 1766 to 1784 (when Wesley himself began ordaining) he assumed that his people would receive the sacraments from Church of England priests on these shores. When that became impossible after 1776, he made the hard choice of allowing his 10,000 to 12,000 followers to remain during those years largely without sacramental ministry, high churchman though he was!

But this dichotomy had to end, and John Wesley thus took the plunge in 1784 and began himself to ordain elders and even bishops. He felt that he was a scriptural *episkopos,* and thus had this right. But even with the establishment of Methodism into a church at the Christmas Conference of 1784, only a few elders were ordained, leaving most of the movement to be led by lay preachers riding throughout the American wilderness. Their ministry was word oriented, and the wild life and spirit of the American frontier seemed more appreciative of that dimension of Christian witness. Liturgy and vestments were quickly reduced to a bare minimum in these conditions.

Thus, for many decades, the identity of Methodism and the traveling preachers of Methodism were centered on the prophetic preaching of the Word, to the detriment of the priestly dimensions of ministry and the sacraments. The ministry of the Word was regarded as a divine calling; a preacher's responsibility and aim was to announce the good news of what God had done in Jesus Christ. The supervision of the maturation of the flock was also included in a man's call, but because he was traveling constantly, this care, in fact, fell on lay leaders of the societies.

The stringent military-like organization of Methodism at this time in the United States seemed to be the most effective means of disseminating the gospel. Wesley's words served as a guide: "My business on earth is, to do what good I can. . . . As to my preaching here, a dispensation of the Gospel is committed to me; and woe is me if I preach not the Gospel, wherever I am in the habitable world."[30] This is to say that Methodism was seen primarily in terms of a movement, with its preachers as the messengers. The priestly ministry that priests in the Church of England had provided in Britain was not really cared for, except by the presiding elders, whose visits to any society or congregation *might* be quarterly and might be less frequent! So Methodism continued to live on in a form that had emerged in a different era and a different milieu. The minister was a preacher, and pastoral ministry was provided primarily by laity or occasionally by a preacher who happened to be present.

As the United States became more settled in the 1840s and 1850s, this situation changed radically, and a constantly growing percentage of ministers began to be appointed to single or possibly two- or three-point charges, rather than extensive circuits. At the same time the length of stay permitted in a single charge was lengthened from two years in 1804 to five years by 1888. In 1900 a maximum stay was done away with. So more of a settled, shepherding ministry became *possible*. Nevertheless, ministers who had understood their primary ministry in terms of preaching continued, even after assuming a more complete pastoral ministry, to view the sacraments, and especially the Lord's Supper, with some suspicion. Any hint of "sacerdotalism" was suspect as well: the ordination of bishops (which Coke and Asbury had assumed and accepted) was early changed to "consecration"; the use of wine in the eucharist was changed to unfermented juice in mid-century. As a "church of the people," Methodism more and more took on the democratic ideals of the culture surrounding it, which generally did not look kindly on "priestcraft."

I have several times alluded to the importance to his movement that Wesley considered continuing relationship with the Church of England. At one point he said that if the Methodists ever left the Church of England, God would leave *them*. He would not leave that Church, and its bishops would not expel him. He understood the need for both prophetic and priestly ministry in one Body.

Methodism in our day is slowly coming to a more complete and wholistic understanding of the priestliness of ministry, in the context of the priestly church. Albert Outler put it thus:

> [Methodism] has never developed—on its own and for itself—the full panoply of bell, book, and candle that goes with being a "proper" church properly self-understood. . . . I suggest that Methodism's unique ecclesiological pattern was really designed to function best *within* an encompassing environment of catholicity (by which I mean what the word meant originally: the effectual and universal Christian *community*). We need a catholic church within which to function as a proper evangelical order of witness and worship, discipline and nurture.[31]

So we have come full circle. It was conjectured at the end of the preceding section that a pervasive individualism had led the concept and exercise of priesthood into deep water, an individualism that assumed direct communication and relation with the divine virtually separate from the church.

The individualism for which we commonly blame the Renaissance or Reformation is deeply ingrained in the thought and practice of the Middle Ages. It produced the tendency to think of the Christian minister as an individual practitioner who brings the grace of God to bear by preaching and sacrament and to think of other ministries as being conducted by a number of other individuals.[32]

The same shortcoming had led Methodism to err in the opposite direction. Its preachers traveled the length and breadth of the country proclaiming grace, but neglecting the corporate expression of the church and its traditional worship in the Lord's Supper. Both extremes had neglected the full pastoral dimensions of the ordained ministry, but for virtually opposite reasons.

Earlier I mentioned the observation of Schillebeeckx: part of the trouble with the Middle Ages development of priesthood was that the pneumatological was separated from the ecclesiological, resulting in a pervasive privatism and individualism, which, in the development of frontier America, both encouraged the individualism already present in church and culture and was further encouraged by it.

The same result was apparent as the Protestant churches in general came to exalt the "pulpits" and the "princes" who occupied them. In a real sense these people (almost always men) became "mediators" between God and ordinary people just as fully as any priestly doctrine gone awry.

Phillips Brooks defined real preaching as "truth through personality."[33] In describing the difference, Richard Baxter wrote: "The priest has no great demand for personality; with the preacher, however, such is not the case. More important than almost anything else is the man himself."[34] This cult of "the man," or exaltation of a person's personality, falls victim to a serious danger in the possible idolatry of the preacher, from which priests are usually spared.

The great P. T. Forsyth, speaking in 1907, wisely observed:

You hear it said, with a great air of religious common sense, that it is the man that the modern age demands in the pulpit, and not his doctrine. It is the man that counts, and not his creed. But this is one of those shallow and plausible half-truths which have the success that always follows when the easy, obvious underpart is blandly offered for the arduous whole. No man has any right in the pulpit in virtue of his personality or manhood in itself, but only in virtue of the sacramental value of his personality for his message. We have no business to worship the elements, which means, in this case, to idolise the preacher. . . . To be ready to accept any kind of message from a magnetic man is to lose the Gospel in mere impressionism. It is to sacrifice the moral in religion to the aesthetic. And it is fatal to the authority either of the pulpit or the Gospel. The Church does not live by its preachers, but by its Word.[35]

How, then, might we restore a needed balance between priest and prophet, between word and sacrament?

Toward a Resolution of Balance

It can be said that, particularly in the ecumenical discussion of ministry, there is a return today to a more corporate understanding of the place of the Christian priesthood/ministry in the church, in which we go back to the days of the early Christian community and forward into the future with new expressions of ancient life, bringing out of God's treasure things new and old. The liturgical movement, with all of its riches, is effectively reminding us of the various dimensions of pastoral ministry, and that minister/priest and people are brought by one Spirit into one Body.[36]

Another dimension of pastoral ministry that is being more appreciated is the ministry of the ordained to the world around the community. Throughout its history the Christian ministry has been concerned for the temporal as well as the spiritual welfare of human beings; the definition of pastoral care that a church historian produced for sixth-century Gaul is still useful here: "Pastoral care of souls is that form of Christian charity exercised from day to day by a corps of consecrated men in (a) maintaining Divine Worship for, (b) communicating Sacramental Life to, (c) providing inspirational guidance for, and (d) procuring material benefits for that portion of mankind officially assigned to its charge."[37]

Community: Flock and Shepherd

In discussing priest and preacher I have noted how both concentrations became one-sided and unbalanced; both styles of ministry became overly individualistic and fell victim to a kind of privatism and individualism that needed correction and balancing by a more corporate understanding and exercise of ministry. In this final section I shall look briefly at the beginnings of a restoration of balance.

I have mentioned frequently in this essay the critical place of community for an authentic understanding and exercise of Christian ministry. The place and nature of this community needs to be central in restoring the right kind of balance, since priesthood in the Roman Catholic tradition seemed to become a privatized offering of sacrifice without the community's genuine participation, and ministry in Protestantism often became so focused on preaching that the church became a group of spectators listening to a learned address.

Perhaps one image to help in a restoration of balance might come to us out of the pastoral language of the Bible. In an article entitled "The Pastoral Image in the New Testament," Prof. John Jansen, of the Austin Theological Seminary in Austin, Texas, mines the extensive riches of biblical thought on this subject in a most helpful manner. He shows how the title shepherd associates the person immediately with Jesus himself. In fact, the title takes us back to our Old Testament roots. God is the Shepherd of Israel (Psalm 80:1). The Shepherd God appoints undershepherds (Psalm 77:20). Prophets look to a time when God will gather the people like a shepherd (Isaiah 40:11).

The newborn Jesus will shepherd his people (Matthew 2:6); the Gospels portray Jesus as a shepherd, seeking lost sheep, laying down his life for the sheep. There is an elasticity here too. Paul Minear reminds us that Jesus is also the lamb and a sheep. Jesus comes to shepherd but identifies himself completely with the flock and becomes a lamb (Acts 8:32; Isaiah 53:7).[38] Jesus sends out his followers as sheep; they can be shepherds, but the shepherds have the same needs as the sheep! Thus the New Testament image of pastoral ministry begins with the pastoral ministry of Jesus, not with questions of church order.[39] This observation is of basic importance.

The New Testament image of 1 Peter 2 develops the theme further. Those who are overseeing (presbyter/bishop) are told to tend or feed the flock, not for gain, but as good examples. There are dangers here as well; sheep are sometimes rather stupid, and a pastor can get into bad habits of assuming the flock does not know very much. There are also some who forget that shepherds lead their flocks through danger and are not satisifed to *drive* them from behind!

So we see that in the passages of the New Testament where pastoral imagery is vital, the specific meaning to be given the function described by the shepherd imagery depends on the specific nature of the community that is the "flock"; the shepherd is to provide whatever is required for the life of the flock. Moreover, later shepherds of the Christian community are to provide for it as does Jesus himself, for he is the model shepherd, the example for his disciples. He remains the great shepherd (Hebrews 13:20).[40]

The fact that Jesus' disciples are both flock and shepherd has many implications. Peter receives the commission to feed the flock (John 21:15). And Acts 20:28 reminds us of the self-understanding of the community as being the flock of Christ. Ephesians 4:11 also reminds us of the power of the pastoral image in the leadership of the early church. Shepherds are also linked to teaching.

Bernard Cooke reminds us well of the vital place of the community/flock:

> Behind the figure of shepherd/flock lies the notion of assembling, of gathering together, of forming the *ekklesia*. The shepherd must be solicitous about the life of each of the flock, but his task is to keep the flock unified, to resist the forces that would tend to disperse the sheep. . . . The various ministries share this common objective of preserving the unity and vitality of the people.[41]

Continuing Points for Discussion

Early in the life of the church the leaders of the community had presided at the eucharist. But as time went on (as described earlier), the link between community and ministry was narrowed down to an inner bond between priesthood and eucharist.[42]

At the center of this narrowing was a hardening understanding of "power" to confect and a mechanical view of the Supper itself, which eventually made of the event a change that the priest, by virtue of priestly power, was effecting. And indeed, some ambiguity on this point remains between the churches. For example, the official United Methodist—Roman Catholic statement on the eucharist contains statements like this: "Our conversations brought out the fact that many United Methodists mean by 'sacrifice' the once-for-all sacrifice of Christ on the cross, while many Roman Catholics think primarily of the sacrifice that the Church has offered down through the centuries, which is that one sacrifice." The statement continues:

> By inter-relating "sacrifice" in terms of memorial, both traditions affirm the once-for-allness of Christ's self offering on the cross. Both affirm that the benefits of his passion and death are present to the faithful now. . . . But the role played by the

Church in offering of this sacrifice remains a problem. The answer to the question of "Who offers what?" is far from clear. United Methodists are not comfortable with such terminology of Vatican II as the eucharist's "perpetuating the sacrifice of the Cross through the centuries."[43]

Nevertheless, the agreements being reached *between* churches on ministry and eucharist are making progress. The progress is built around a changing notion of community and in a keeping together of word and sacrament as one event. Bishop FitzSimmons Allison puts it well: "If eucharist is spoken of as sacrifice, it must be understood as a sacrifice in which . . . we do not offer Christ but in which Christ unites us with himself in the self-offering of the life that was obedient unto death, yea the death of the Cross."[44]

Most churches (including the Roman Catholic and Anglican communion) are now using representative language to speak of the ordained person's relationship to the community in their ecumenical agreements. That is to say, the priest does not make a sacrifice as the older *sacerdos* was thought to do, but rather re-presents that event as elder of the people, the church, of that whole wider priesthood; he or she is a representative person of this holy people, the Body of Christ. So here, too, community offers us hope of moving together.

Another point for discussion is the relation of preaching to the Supper. It is more and more agreed now that word and sacrament are inseparable. Ordained ministry relates Christians to that once-for-all sacrifice of Christ by the preaching of the Word, the good news.

As in the text from Paul (Rom. 15:16), "the priestly service of the gospel of God" is the function and purpose of this ministry. And *hiereus* here is not used to describe Christian ministry, but rather is used to describe the function of the Gospel. It is the Gospel that mediates and relates us to Christ. The ministry does so as it is a servant of this Word. . . . As the presbyter presides at the holy table the once-for-all sacrifice is presented in word and action, and this body, the Church, is united anew with its head in his sacrifice.[45]

Thus both the priest and the preacher need to serve in relation to, not in isolation from, the apostolic community in its priestly service to God. And this priestly ministry also needs to find expression in our manner of life in the world. We are not our own—we were bought with a price, and in our service, whatever it be, we present our souls and bodies, the worship of our hearts and minds, in our sacrifice of praise to the world.[46]

A bringing together of priestly and prophetic and pastoral can be seen in Paul's ministry—his approach can inform ours. Even though Paul was hostile to the priestly party (Sadducees), he uses hieratic imagery constantly for his own ministry. He rejoices in giving priestly and spiritual service to God by preaching the gospel of His Son (Romans 1:9) and compares his work to the liturgy offered by priests; he brings his Gentile converts as a sacred offering (Romans 15:16). He sees himself as a libation (Philippians 2:17). In a bold statement he speaks: "In my flesh I complete what is lacking in Christ's afflictions for the sake of his body [Col. 1:24]."

These reminders of Paul's language make clear that the apostolic minister offers his or her work and suffering on behalf of the church as a gift to God, a kind of self-offering. And this brings us back to the shepherd/lamb/flock motif being reincarnated in the Christian minister/priest.

How can the church continually recast its ministry in an attempt to remain both obedient to its chief Shepherd and yet in communication with the world around it? Because the Shepherd in scriptures is also the flock, and the flock all have shepherding (and therefore sacrificial) responsibilities, a balanced way to the future appears.

The basis of this way must be built on the need for any minister, in any age, in word, deed, and, above all, person, to embody the Christ. Probably the pastoral language of the

Bible is still our most authentic and enduring basis. The true pastor tends, feeds, and cares for the sheep. This includes the full gamut of pastoral roles, leading the flock in being for the world and in praising God.

As I have tried to show, the whole Christian community is priestly. In everything it does it bears witness to the presence of Christ, it makes present Christ's concern for the salvation of human beings. Thus the community is a living sacrifice in which Christ's sacrificial self-gift is made present to humans.[47] As Christ is sacrament making God present in the world, so the church is sacramental, making Christ present by nurturing human community. The whole community is also prophetic, speaking, hearing, and acting the healing word.

Within this flock some are called to give special sacramental expression to Christ's priestly action of Passover so that the entire community can celebrate more authentically and fully its priestly character.[48] This sacramental expression is proclamation of the Word of Christ's death and resurrection—through words and through eucharistic action, which itself is word.

But it is the church in which the central acts take place. Thus, for example, the *Baptism, Eucharist, and Ministry* agreement of the World Council of Churches, the most broadly based ecumenical agreement in history, in its section on the eucharist, says:

> The *anamnesis* in which Christ acts through the joyful celebration of his Church . . . (para. 7)
> The Church, gratefully recalling God's mighty acts of redemption, beseeches God to give the benefits of these acts to every human being. In thanksgiving and intercession, the Church is united with the Son, its great High Priest and Intercessor.[49]

Such phrases occur quite often; they remind us of the dynamic nature of emerging understanding, of the centrality of

Christ, and of the central place given to the church in which the *Spirit* acts.

A Warning

Urban Holmes III, in *The Future Shape of Ministry*, quotes Killian McDonnell to the effect that the "formation of the doctrine of ministry in the Roman Catholic Church was the result of a theological reflection on pastoral needs."[50] The same can be said with more or less certainty about other churches as well—ministry emerged in a context, to fill perceived needs. In the mid-1950s three scholars did a thorough piece of research into what model of pastoral ministry was emerging in American culture in Protestantism. These three (H. Richard Niebuhr, Daniel D. Williams, and James Gustafson) entitled their study *The Purpose of the Church and Its Ministry*. The work described the concept of minister that was becoming most widely accepted; they encapsulated their description with the title "pastoral director."

In a trenchant critique of the trend Niebuhr had described, Robert Paul felt that within this "job description" of the minister of that time, the "pastor" was getting short shrift and the "director" role was predominant. It was, he concluded, another instance of the culture exercising more influence on a ministerial form than either the church or the Bible.[51] In agreeing that the church always tries to conceptualize its ministry in terms of the times, one must always take care that it does not emerge as a "captive" to the times.

Conclusion

There is hope in our day that as the churches, in their ecumenical agreements, are reaching back to the early history of the church, they are finding a more pastoral and complete, and thus authentic, image of the ordained person's ministry.

Subsequent essays in this book will look at some of these agreements, and therefore I shall not try to describe them.

There are lessons to be learned from this history. There are dangers on both sides: by overemphasizing power or juridicial categories, the church developed a legalism more binding than the old; also, a preacher in isolation from the acted word, from the hearing and acting community, easily falls victim to delusions of grandeur or tyranny.

Another pair would be these: It was not the best approach to attempt to reproduce an Old Testament priesthood, since Christ's sacrifice is sufficient once for all, and nothing can or need be added to it. But word without the priestly action of the entire community (and the leader as well) leads to aberrations.

Perhaps more important, on the positive learning side, we in the church have come to understand much anew, or perhaps better, again. Thus we are holding together again prophet and priest and pastor and keeping Word and Sacrament together as parts of one whole. We are learning again that Spirit and church must be kept together as well, so that "enthusiasm" on the one side and dry ecclesiasticism on the other may be avoided. And finally, we are again hearing the vital need to keep together individual and community, thus giving us an opportunity once again to recapture our communal Hebraic roots in a reinvigorated community in Christ.

Who is the pastoral priest/prophet? This person must incarnate in his or her person the spirit of the church as a consecrated ministry. In a peculiar sense this person bears the title "man (or woman) of God," for that life has been publicly consecrated to the service of the gospel (1 Timothy 6:11; 2 Timothy 3:17). This person stands as a public reminder to every Christian that he or she belongs to God.[52]

May it be so.

CHAPTER 3

The Priestly Authority of Paul

Dale Moody

WHEN THE QUESTION OF PRIESTLY AUTHORITY IS RAISED for any person or group, the meaning of "priestly" is first to the fore. Here I use it to describe the function of one person or group that is supposed to have special access to God on behalf of another person or group. This seems clear enough in the theophany of Sinai when God says to Israel: "Now therefore, if you will obey my voice and keep my covenant, you shall be my own possession among all peoples; . . . and you shall be to me a kingdom of priests and a holy nation [Exod. 19:5–6]."

The choice of Moses as a special person with special access to God was a considerable problem for Israel in the later priestly tradition. The story of the punishment of Miriam, the older sister of Moses, with leprosy for challenging this special relationship of her younger brother Moses was told to reinforce this ancient belief (Numbers 12:1–16). The rebellion of Korah, who led some subordinate Levites to revolt against the

---

Dale Moody, D.Th., Ph.D., before retirement was Joseph Emerson Brown Professor of Christian Theology, Southern Baptist Theological Seminary, Louisville, Kentucky.

priestly order of Aaron, resulted in 250 rebels being swallowed up in Sheol (Numbers 16:1–50). This "affair of Korah" became a standard story to reinforce priestly authority (Jude 11).

Authority was believed to reside in the person or group chosen especially by God. This was most conspicuous in the words and deeds of Jesus (Mark 2:1–12), but it could be given also to the apostles (Mark 3:15). That is the meaning of the Greek word *exousia*, that which belongs to the very being of a person. The Gospel of Luke gives special emphasis to this special quality of the Spirit in Jesus (Luke 4:1–44), and the same Luke is believed to be behind the teaching in Acts that allows for apostolic authority to be transferred to the deacons of Jerusalem (Act 6:1–6) and later to the elders in the churches founded by Barnabas and Paul (Acts 14:23). Recent discussions have turned to Luke as the source for the charismatic function of the laying on of hands by the elders as well as by Paul in the Pastoral Epistles (1 Timothy 4:14; 2 Timothy 1:7). At least Luke *alone* is said to be with Paul in his last days (2 Timothy 4:11). But more about this debated issue later. The transfer of priestly authority today really depends on the validity of the theory of apostolic succession through the centuries or the claims of direct access to God through some special relation. Charles H. Spurgeon was so sure of this special relationship to God that he looked with contempt on the theory of apostolic succession through ordination. To him, the practice he observed in the Church of England led him to refuse the ordination, which he regarded as putting empty hands on empty heads. This is frequently the root of conflict between new cult and old church.

The priestly authority of Paul was apostolic authority. One view of priestly authority today is based on the theory of apostolic succession transmitted by ordination, but priestly authority, based on experience and expertise, is also claimed by others and accepted by the others. Paul's authority rested primarily on this second source (Galatians 1:11–22). The validity of this second claim has always been a challenge to institutional authority.

Paul's priestly authority resided in (a) his apostolic message (1 Corinthians 4), (b) his apostolic ministry (1 Corinthians 9), and (c) his apostolic mission (Romans 15). A careful study of these three activities and passages provides a robust picture of the nature and forms of priestly authority.

Priestly Authority in Paul's Apostolic Message

Paul's apostolic message denotes the apostle as a servant (1 Corinthians 4:1–5), as a fool (4:6–13), and as a father (4:14–21). *The model of a servant* is that of *hyperetas,* literally under-rowers, subordinate to the Christ in command. In Greek culture this was a sign of weakness, not a characteristic of great men (Plato, *Laws* 6.774c). It is a term used in other New Testament passages for attendants in the synagogue (Luke 4:20; Acts 13:5). The stress on subordination and responsibility to a superior is different from the word *diakonoi,* which Paul ascribes to all ministers of the New Covenant in Christ (1 Corinthians 3:5).

As servant *(hyperetas),* Paul describes himself as the steward *(oikonomos)* of the mysteries of God. These mysteries include all that has been revealed by the Spirit (1 Corinthians 2:7–10), not only the meaning of the so-called sacraments of the church. These mysteries are the secrets of those initiated into the things of the Spirit (1 Corinthians 2:7). Mystery is from *mustes,* an initiate, from *mueo,* meaning to blink or wink.

The term is used also of the kingdom of God (Matthew 13:11) and of God (1 Corinthians 4:1). In Ephesians the word is applied to God's will (1:9), to Christ (3:4), and to the gospel (6:19). The Pastorals use the word to describe the faith (1 Timothy 3:9) and the Christian religion as a whole (1 Timothy 3:16). There is no way to reduce the mysteries of God to the wisdom of the natural person. It is all foolishness to him or her

(1 Corinthians 2:14). Paul says "man" and "him." (His language had not been "desexed.") The mysteries belong to the very depths of God and have meaning to those who possess the Spirit of God. Even those who possess the Spirit as mere babes are able to drink only the milk. Such solid food is not digestible by those living as factions in the body of Christ (1 Corinthians 3:1–3).

The primary qualification of the stewards of the mysteries is faithfulness. But who is to be the judge of one's faithfulness? Paul's answer is that God is the judge. The same God who controls the eschatological future when the hidden things of darkness will be brought into light. Human standards in the present age are rejected lest the apostle become a person directed by others. That, for Paul, is the lowest standard of faithfulness. Paul said: "But with me it is a very small thing that I should be judged by you or by any human court. I do not even judge myself [1 Cor. 4:3]."

The criterion of self-judgment seems far more reliable than that of social pressure. Martyrs have died, paying a terrible price for freedom of conscience, and the model for all is none other than Jesus Christ. For the disciples and apostles of Christ the last chapter has not been written. The final word on faithfulness remains in the future. Paul says of that day: "I am not aware of anything against myself, but I am not thereby acquitted. It is the Lord who judges me. Therefore do not pronounce judgment before the time, before the Lord comes, who will bring to light the things now hidden in darkness and will disclose the purposes of the heart. Then every man will receive his commendation from God [1 Cor. 4:4–5]."

Paul's Gnostic opponents thought that they had already reached perfection, but they were rootless wonders who detached themselves from the scriptures of the Old Testament or possibly a previous letter of Paul (1 Corinthians 5:9). The Revised Standard Version does not hesitate to adopt the "according to scripture" principle. Most of all, a reminder of the grace of God takes the puff out of Paul's opponents' pretense.

Three questions expose the proud. First: "Who sees anything different in you?" Second: "What have you that you did not receive?" And the third question is the final rebuke: "If then you received it, why do you boast as if it were not a gift? [1 Cor. 4:7]."

The model of a fool contrasts the "realized eschatology" of this Gnostic opponent with the "realistic eschatology" of the apostolic faith. In biting sarcasm and irony the apostle says: "Already you are filled! Already you have become rich! Without us you have become kings! And would that you did reign, so that we might share the rule with you! [1 Cor. 4:8]." They seemed to think they had already brought in the reign of God with corporate headquarters in Corinth. They had forgotten that the reign of God is an inheritance of the future that brings all things present under judgment (1 Corinthians 6:9f.; 15:50). God's rule was present in the power of the Spirit but not in the glory of triumphalism (1 Corinthians 4:20; Romans 14:17; Colossians 1:13; Ephesians 5:5).

The perils, polarities, and paradoxes of this mortal life are graphically displayed as in a triumphal procession in which the rulers of this present age exhibit their trophies and captives. "For I think that God has exhibited us apostles as last of all, like men sentenced to death; because we have become a spectacle to the world, to angels and to men [1 Cor. 4:9]." Our word theater is derived from the word translated "spectacle." The apostles are pictured as victims destined to die in arenas of the world. It is indeed existence unto death, but beyond is the gift of immortality. Paul rejected the Greek view of *natural* immortality, but he used immortality as a gift from God, as a synonym for life (1 Corinthians 15:54; 2 Corinthians 5:4).

The paradox of it all for Paul is: "We are fools for Christ's sake, but you are wise in Christ. We are weak, but you are strong. You are held in honor, but we in disrepute [1 Cor. 4:10]." This is the paradox of pride that will perish at the end.

Realistic eschatology stands in vivid contrast to the realized eschatology of Paul's Gnostic opponents. "To the present hour we hunger and thirst, we are ill-clad and buffeted and homeless, and we labor, working with our own hands. When reviled, we bless; when persecuted, we endure; when slandered, we try to conciliate; we have become, and are now, as the refuse of the world, the offscouring of all things [1 Cor. 4:11–13]."

While still in Ephesus Paul spoke of his hardships in more detail. This is the so-called *Narranrede*, "Fool's Speech" (2 Corinthians 11:1—12:13).[1] His opponents are blasted as "superlative apostles" (2 Corinthians 11:5), even "false apostles, deceitful [workers], disguising themselves as apostles of Christ [11:13]." They belong to those who are "false brethren" (11:26). All this is his response to any challenge to his apostolic message and his status as an apostle.

Paul describes his own boasting as foolishness (11:16). Five times he repeats the model of his life as that of a "fool" (11:16f., 21; 12:6, 11). His list of perils is expanded as he writes from Ephesus, and he restates the perils when in Macedonia (2 Corinthians 6:3–10). His authority as an apostle is undergirded by the marks of suffering in this present age with the apostolic hope that the age of glory will follow in the future.

The model of a father increases the claims of priestly authority (1 Corinthians 4:14–21). Here the contrast is between the thousands of pedagogues on the one hand and Paul who begat them by the preaching of the gospel on the other. That is why the Corinthian believers are admonished as his "beloved children" (4:14). As his children already they are called to be imitators of him in belief and in behavior. Such admonition is characteristic of Paul's relation to his readers (1 Thessalonians 5:12, 14; 2 Thessalonians 2:15; Romans 15:14; Colossians 1:28; 3:16). Positive correction is an expression of both authority and love. Tutors serve as guardians, not as parents. Paul does not use his relation to them as if he regenerated them. That was done "through the gospel." The function as father to children is not used as a title. He does not contradict the teaching of Jesus that forbade calling a man father (Matthew 23:9).

Their imitation of Paul is to be as he imitated Christ. This again is a standard teaching in Paul's letters. The Thessalonians became examples in Macedonia (1 Thessalonians 1:6), but they had become also "imitators of the churches of God in Christ Jesus which are in Judea [1 Thess. 2:14]." In this way the Thessalonians are called on to imitate Paul and his associates (2 Thessalonians 3:7, 9). To the Philippians he says: "Brethren, join in imitating me, and mark those who so live as you have an example in us [3:17]." There is no reason why they could not imitate Christ directly had they known the historical Jesus, but as it is they are to imitate those who imitate Christ.

Timothy is singled out as Paul's "beloved and faithful child in the Lord [1 Cor. 4:17]." He could remind them by precept and example of Paul's imitation of Christ. Some of Paul's associates were not so faithful. To the Philippians he could say: "But Timothy's worth you know, how as a son with a father he has served with me in the gospel [2:22]."

Discipline is included in this fatherly relation. Like many modern Christians, the Corinthians were doing much talking, so they needed to be reminded that "the kingdom of God does not consist in talk but in power [1 Cor. 4:20]." To those puffed up with pride he gave the option of the rod *(rabdos)* of discipline or "love in a spirit of gentleness [1 Cor. 4:21]."

Priestly Authority in Paul's Apostolic Ministry

Paul's apostolic ministry exemplifies priestly authority in several ways, especially in 1 Corinthians 9. In a review of his apostolic rights, which he, in the end, rejects, Paul first appeals to logic (9:1–7). His eschatological freedom, anchored in the future, is again at the fore. In four questions the foundations are laid: "Am I not free? Am I not an apostle?

Have I not seen Jesus our Lord? Are not you my workmanship in the Lord? [9:1]." The freedom of the future rests on the resurrection of the Lord, and the major evidence for his resurrection is found in his appearances after his death and resurrection.

The *locus classicus* for the appearances of the resurrected Jesus is 1 Corinthians 15:3–8. Unfortunately, the Authorized (King James) Version leaves room for Gnostic subjectivism by the translation of "was seen" (15:5–7). The Revised Standard Version reads:

> For I delivered to you as of first importance what I also received, that Christ died for our sins in accordance with the scriptures, that he was buried, that he was raised on the third day in accordance with the scriptures, and that he appeared to Cephas, then to the twelve. Then he appeared to more than five hundred brethren at one time, most of whom are still alive, though some have fallen asleep. Then he appeared to James, then to all the apostles. Last of all, as to one untimely born, he appeared also to me.

The appearances to Mary Magdalene, the women, Cleopas and his companion, Thomas, and seven of his disciples by the Sea of Tiberius are not mentioned by Paul, but they are independent witnesses to the appearances. In and near Jerusalem and in Galilee over a period of six Sundays these were celebrated in the early church. Here I must give thanks to Pierre Benoit, the great Dominican scholar of *Ecole Biblique* in Jerusalem, for the many hours we have spent together discussing the historical and geographical question related to the appearances. His full-day lecture "In Search of Emmaus" remains in my memory as a bulwark against Rudolf Bultmann and his school, who reduce the appearances to mythology.[2] The appearances have enough claim to validity for the Jewish scholar David Flusser to subscribe to Paul's witness in 1 Corinthians 15:3–8.[3] If Jesus was raised from the dead and died no more, the whole Christian future follows logically. If Jesus Christ never died again, he must be alive. When and if a

Messiah appears in the future, he will most likely be Jesus returning according to his promise. This is the key to Paul's priestly authority in his apostolic ministry.

A second claim to apostolic authority rests on Paul's "workmanship" plus the fact of the Corinthian community of faith (1 Corinthians 9:1). This was indeed "the seal" of his apostleship in the Lord. As Paul relates his "rights" in defense of his apostleship, his first claim is that he has the right to be supported. The word for "right" is the word often translated "authority" *(exousia)*. Indeed he (and Barnabas) had the right to refrain from working for a living and to be accompanied by a wife. One thinks what a good wife Phoebe the deacon would have made for Paul (Romans 16:1f.). Here tradition since Jerome should be corrected with scripture. Not only were other apostles married, but special emphasis is given to "the brothers of the Lord and Cephas [1 Cor. 9:5]." Efforts to explain away James, Joseph, Simon, and Judas, along with at least two sisters, by some Roman Catholic scholars show as much strain as the attacks on the appearances of Jesus after his death and resurrection. It is well that *The New Oxford Annotated Bible* states both Roman Catholic and Protestant views on Mark 3:31f.; Matthew 1:25; Luke 2:7; 8:19f.; John 2:12; 7:3, 5; Acts 1:14, Galatians 1:9, as well as on 1 Corinthians 9:5, but this seems clearly a clash between scripture and tradition, and this is a hindrance to Christian unity.

I make no quarrel with the claim that the Bishop of Rome is a logical choice to sit in the "chair of Peter." It should be the center for Christian unity, but there should be no evasion of Cephas (Simon Peter) being a married man. It has been revealed that the pontificate of Pope Pius XII, one of the major popes of modern times, was greatly influenced by a gifted woman who lived with him. Without any suggestion of scandal, a beautiful and intelligent Bavarian peasant nun, Josephine Lehnert, known as Sister Pascalina, after years of service for Pacelli in Germany, lived in the Vatican with Pacelli, after he became Pius XII, for almost twenty years and was faithful and devoted to him until his death. Of course there were those who referred to her sarcastically as "La Popessa" or the "German general" because of her strong influence on Pope Pius XII. The only unbecoming things that developed seemed to relate to prelates who tried to overcome her influence. The whole relation seemed as holy as that which must have existed between Jesus and Mary Magdalene or Paul and deacon Phoebe.[4]

But to return to Paul's authority, three questions illustrate the right to refrain from secular work while in the apostolic ministry. "Who serves as a soldier at his own expense? Who plants a vineyard without eating any of its fruit? Who tends a flock without getting some of the milk? [1 Cor. 9:9]."

A second appeal for Paul's rights in his apostolic ministry is to the law of Moses. The opening question is: "Do I say this on human authority? [1 Cor. 9:8]." Deuteronomy 25:4 was used to justify Paul's right to expect support. "You shall not muzzle an ox when it is treading out the grain [1 Cor. 9:9]." This kindness and fairness to animals illustrates how Old Testament scripture was used to justify support not only for the apostle Paul, but also for other official ministers.

The same Deuteronomic law is joined with a saying of Jesus in Matthew 10:10 and Luke 10:7, a so-called Q saying. To support the plea for a double honorarium for elders who rule well, "especially those who labor in preaching and teaching [1 Tim. 5:17]," the Q saying in Matthew 10:10 and Luke 10:7 says: "The laborer deserves his wages [1 Tim. 5:18]." Ruling and teaching elders became the first successors to the apostles in the official ministry of the New Testament; 1 Peter 5:1 reflects the belief in Rome in which Peter is regarded "as a fellow elder," but 1 Timothy 3:1 has the "office of bishop," a presiding elder in Ephesus. This was the step that led to the threefold ministry of deacons, elders, and the bishop that is so clear in the letters of Ignatius of Antioch at the beginning of the second century.

Even in the congregationalism of modern Baptist churches

the belief is strong for supporting those who rule and teach as elders, now called pastors. Once while preaching to a pastorless congregation in the historic Bluegrass region of Kentucky, I bore down hard against churches that "muzzle the ox." The response of one prosperous farmer was mixed. He agreed that the church should do better in "paying the preacher," but he wanted me to know that one ox I recommended didn't tread out any grain. Their next pastor was good at separating the wheat from the chaff so he never again had any problem with ministerial support.

Returning to the theme of the priestly authority of Paul, the application of the law about oxen to the apostolic ministry is interesting.

> Is it for oxen that God is concerned? Does he not speak entirely for our sake? It was written for our sake, because the [plower] should plow in hope and the thresher thresh in hope of a share in the crop. If we have sown spiritual good among you, is it too much if we reap your material benefits? If others share this rightful claim upon you, do not we still more? (1 Cor. 9:9–12)

The appeal to the service of the Levites in the temple is one of the strongest for the priestly authority of Paul (1 Corinthians 9:12–14). Levites were assistants to the temple priests in the temple. Paul argues that he has the right or authority to do among the churches what the Levites did in the temple. The analogy is most instructive for the understanding of priestly authority. He asks: "Do you not know that those who are employed in the temple service get their food from the temple, and those who serve at the altar share in the sacrificial offerings? In the same way, the Lord commanded that those who proclaim the gospel should get their living by the gospel [1 Cor. 9:13–14]."

In the effort to restore the apostolic ministry in a frontier situation, the Baptists of the Bluegrass, along with Presbyterians, Methodists, and Disciples, are interesting and instructive. The Do-Nothing Baptist John Taylor (1752–1835), in his *Thoughts on Missions* (1820), was strongly opposed to the collection of funds by Luther Rice for the missionary work by Adoniram Judson in Burma. Strangely enough, Taylor had been a leader in the evangelism of The Great Revival in 1801 and afterward. The big problem seemed to be that Luther Rice was a gifted and cultured Yankee and Taylor was a rugged and intelligent frontiersman.

There were also those who gave generously to missions but objected to resident pastors being paid. The most notable example was the wealthy Elijah Craig, one of three brothers in the Craig clan. His pamphlet on "A Few Remarks on the Errors That Are Maintained in Christian Churches of the Present Day" (1801) argued that the local clergy should "travel the same thorny way as the laity, of labour, cares of this life, etc."[5] With his 4,000 acres, eleven horses, thirty-two slaves, and lucrative sale of Bourbon whiskey, which he invented, Craig had few "cares of this life." The clergy of today give thanks that the "crisis with Craig" has not muzzled the ox in the beautiful Bluegrass.

Returning again to the priestly authority of Paul, it may be summarized by saying that Paul's apostolic *exousia* (right, authority) was renounced as he preached the gospel in Corinth. His preaching was a holy compulsion that gave him no option. He said: "For necessity is laid upon me. Woe to me if I do not preach the gospel! [1 Cor. 9:16]."

Priestly Authority in Paul's Apostolic Mission

In the days leading up to the Vatican Council II, 1962–65, Oscar Cullmann suggested that Christian unity could be expressed between Catholics and Protestants by the institution of a reciprocal collection between them. As far as I know this was never fully realized, although many individuals and congregations responded, but many more were impressed that a first-rate New Testament scholar really believed in the practical application of what he knew so well.[6] Soon afterward

Keith F. Nickle, a student under Cullman's supervision, submitted a doctoral dissertation on *The Collection: A Study in Paul's Strategy*.[7] This collection is specifically called "the priestly service of the gospel of God" by the apostle Paul himself (Romans 15:16).

The first reference to this collection seems to be the well-known words often quoted in part before the collection or offering in modern churches. "Now concerning the contribution for the saints: as I directed the churches of Galatia, so you also are to do. On the first day of every week, each of you is to put something aside and store it up, as he may prosper, so that contributions need not be made when I come [1 Cor. 16:1–2]." Thus began what was to become one of the strongest elements in free church worship to this day.

The mother church of Jerusalem had practiced the community of goods much as the Qumran community had previously. This was known as the *koinonia* (Acts 2:42), in which "all who believed were together and had all things in common [*koina*, Acts 2:44]." Among them was a certain Joseph, a Levite, who was called Barnabas by the apostles and is interpreted as "Son of encouragement" (Acts 4:36). This native of Cypess "sold a field which belonged to him, and brought the money and laid it at the apostles' feet [Acts 4:37]." It is no wonder that the first great Latin theologian, Tertullian of Carthage, at the beginning of the third century, expressed no doubt that this "Son of encouragement" or exhortation was the author of Hebrews, called a "word of exhortation" (Hebrews 13:22), the first Christology of priesthood in Christian literature (see Tertullian, *On Modesty*, ch. 20).

Furthermore, during the great famine about A.D. 46, it was this Barnabas, along with Saul (later Paul), who was chosen to send the relief from Antioch to Jerusalem (Acts 11:27–30). It is probable that this stimulated the hope for the great collection, mentioned in all of Paul's four longest letters. It is a complicated historical question, but many believe that the six-year collection took place between the sabbatical years A.D. 49 and

55 and that it resulted from the promise "to remember the poor" made by Barnabas and Paul at the Jerusalem Council in A.D. 49 (Galatins 2:10). It is also probable that the instruction in Galatians 6:6 has reference to this collection: "Let him who is taught the word share all good things with him who teaches."

It is certain that 2 Corinthians 8—9 is concerned with this manifestation of the grace of God in the generosity of giving. Liberality has oddly become a term of reproach in our reactionary culture, but for Paul, it was the "gracious work" of God in giving (2 Corinthians 8:1–7). In these days when many congregations spend enormous amounts of money on building programs and give less and less to the relief of the poor and to the promotion of world missions, there is a distinct distortion of priorities. As the most generous church in Texas was giving to the Cooperative Program of Southern Baptists $1 million for the year, another church was putting $35 million into a building program. That sort of activity appropriately has been called an "edifice complex." It has begun to look like the Christianity of South America, with elaborate displays of wealth in cathedrals in the midst of sprawling ghettos of poverty.

For Paul, liberality was an imitation of Christ. He could say: "For you know the grace of our Lord Jesus Christ, that though he was rich, yet for your sake he became poor, so that by his poverty you might become rich [2 Cor. 8:9]." Paul's was a plea for "equality" between the rich and the poor (2 Corinthians 8:13–15). This work of grace was especially manifested in the churches of Macedonia. It is not clear who was "the brother who is famous among all the churches for his preaching of the gospel [2 Co. 8:18]," but it is possibly Luke, who would later write Luke-Acts without telling readers the name of the author. No wonder Paul called him "the beloved physician" (Colossians 4:14). Our modern "Corinthian" churches should hear the call to imitate Christ and the Macedonians (2 Corinthians 9:1–15). God is indeed a giving God, a God of grace, who supplied the wants of the needy saints (2 Corinthians 9:6–15): "Thanks be to God for his inexpressible gift! [2 Cor. 9:15]."

As the Jerusalem church had chosen seven men to distribute the goods there, so Paul had seven messengers (apostles) among Gentile churches appointed to take the collection to the poor saints in Jerusalem. Evidence of Paul's commitment to the collection is revealed by his declaration before Governor Felix that he was arrested when he came to bring "alms and offerings" to his own nation that he deeply loved (Acts 24:17).

This was anticipated as he wrote his Letter to the Romans, about A.D. 55, from Corinth, shortly before he and the Gentile seven set out on their mission to Jerusalem. In this role he thought of himself as a *leitourgos* (a priestly minister) who was offering a "priestly service" *(hierourgounta)* to God (Romans 15:16). A conservative Protestant scholar, James Denney, said that the term *leitourgos* "derives from the context the priestly associations often attach to it in the LXX." To this A.T. Robertson adds the comment on *hierourgounta:* "It means to work in sacred things, to minister as a priest."[8]

Confirmation of Paul as a true apostle with authority and miraculous power is mentioned in all four of the major letters. In 1 Corinthians 12:9–10 gifts of healing and miracles are among the spiritual gifts given to the church as the body of Christ on earth. The Galatians (3:5) are asked: "Does he who supplies the Spirit to you and works miracles among you do so by works of the law, or by hearing with faith?" It is obvious that miracles confirmed his preaching of the righteousness or justification that is received by faith. Signs and wonders and mighty works are used in 2 Corinthians 12:12 to support his claim to be a "true apostle" with authority from Christ.

As Paul looks back on his apostolic mission in the East and anticipates a mission to the West, he says:

For I will not venture to speak of anything except what Christ has wrought through me to win obedience from the Gentiles, by word and deed, by the power of signs and wonders, by the power of the Holy Spirit, so that from Jerusalem and as far round as Illyricum I have surely preached the gospel of Christ, thus making it my ambition to preach the gospel, not where Christ has already been named, lest I build on another man's foundation. (Rom. 15:18–20)

The other man's foundation was perhaps the work of Peter. It is simply not true to say Paul had no room for belief in miracles. They confirmed him as a true apostle.

The use of the language of priestly sacrifice in the so-called Pastoral Epistles will be challenged by some, so a few words of clarification on Paul's ministry beyond Rome are offered. Jack Finegan's thorough study of this debated issue is generally accepted here. Paul's purpose in going to Rome was to impart to them "some spiritual gift" (Romans 1:11) and for them to speed him on his way to Spain (Romans 15:24; see also Acts 19:21). Clement of Rome, writing to Corinth about A.D. 95, indicates that Paul did just that before he and Peter died the death of martyrs around January A.D. 68, before the suicide of the playboy Emperor Nero (1 Clem. 5; see also Eusebius, *H.E.* 2.2.2.2). If he arrived in Rome in A.D. 57–58 and departed in A.D. 59–60, as much evidence and tradition indicate, there was plenty of time for him to have an apostolic mission to Spain, A.D. 59–65, from Tarraco near Barcelona to Gades (Cadiz) in southwest Spain.

Taking the suggestions in the Pastorals he could have returned to the Eastern Empire to leave Titus in Crete (Titus 1:5, from Philippi) and Timothy in Ephesus (1 Timothy 1:3, from Nicopolis) and spend the winter of A.D. 66–67 in the historic and beautiful area of Nicopolis (Titus 3:12), across the bay from Actium, where one of the major battles of history was fought in 31 B.C. It was there that Octavian defeated Mark Anthony and Cleopatra. On his return to Troas, he was perhaps arrested and taken back to Rome in A.D. 67, before his execution in January A.D. 68, or possibly late 67 (2 Timothy 4:9–18, from Rome).[9]

The least that can be said is that Paul planned to go to both Rome and Spain when he sent his Letter to the Romans, perhaps by Phoebe, after his last visit to Jerusalem. It is not probable that the plans were changed by his arrest in Jerusalem, in A.D. 55, and the two years as a prisoner in Caesarea (Acts 24:27), where his so-called Prison Letters (Philippians, Colossians, Philemon, and Ephesians) were composed.

I have, for the most part, confined this discussion on priestly authority to the big four Epistles that all scholars seem to agree are genuinely Pauline, but other authorities argue for the authenticity of both the Prison Epistles of Philippians, Colossians, Philemon, and Ephesians and for the Pastoral Epistles of Titus and 1 and 2 Timothy. In all these writings Paul had either Timothy or Luke as secretary. That is why their language of priestly sacrifice supplements the idea of priestly authority.

Soon after Paul's imprisonment began, perhaps in Caesarea, A.D. 55, the Philippian letter was written. Knowing that it was possible that his imprisonment might lead to a martyr's death, he spoke of it as "gain" and a departure to be with Christ, which would be "far better" (1:23). "Even if I am to be poured out as a libation upon the sacrificial offering of your faith, I am glad and rejoice with you all [2:17]." This libation has the background of the priestly sacrifices offered daily in the temple of Jerusalem where Paul almost lost his life (cf. Exodus 29:38–41). Ernst Lohmeyer appropriately has called this a theology of martyrdom![10]

Before the end of this two-year imprisonment Paul speaks of his suffering as vicarious. "Now I rejoice in my sufferings for your sake, and in my flesh I complete what is lacking in Christ's afflictions for the sake of his body, that is, the church [Col. 1:24]." His claim of apostolic authority follows immediately (1:25–27). This echoes the language used earlier, in 2 Corinthians 1:5, 4:10. The rash argument that denies Paul's relation to the Colossian letter is just so much critical dogmatism.[11]

Furthermore, to declare that there was no "letter from Laodicea" (Colossians 4:16) that was to be exchanged for the letter to the Colossians is to resort to the kind of high-handed scholarship that hampers historical research. Little attention is paid to the great work of Ernst Lohmeyer, who died a martyr's death at the hands of German Nazis.

Some of the oldest manuscripts do not have the Greek words for "in Ephesus" *(en Epheso)* in 1:1, and this has led to the view that Ephesians is the letter to and from Laodicea. Ernst Lohmeyer did not live to publish his study of Ephesians, but Oscar Cullmann, his close friend, has assured me that he believed all the Prison Epistles were written from Caesarea. The scribe for Ephesians and the Pastoral Epistles was perhaps Luke (2 Timothy 4:11). In Luke-Acts, Luke also never mentions himself as the secretary. Timothy always put his name at the beginning of letters in which he had a hand (1 and 2 Thessalonians, 2 Corinthians, Philippians, Colossians, and Philemon).

The language of priestly sacrifice and apostolic authority continues in the letter to Laodicea (Ephesians). The temple of Jerusalem is the framework for the *Shalom* Hymn in Ephesians 2:14–18. This peace is in the language of Leviticus 1—7, especially the fellowship offering (Leviticus 1—7; 7:11–34). Romans 3:25 used the Day of Atonement as the type of God's sacrifice of Christ. There is increasing support for the view that Paul was released from house arrest in Rome around A.D. 60 and that he made a fourth missionary journey, this time to Spain.[12]

After his second Roman arrest, perhaps in Troas in A.D. 67, Paul was returned to Rome, where Nero had him beheaded in the very year that Nero committed suicide and Paul made his "departure" to be with the living Christ. The priestly type here is that of the drink offering poured out around the base of the altar (Numbers 15:1–2; 28:7, 24). His victorious words from Rome were: "For I am already on the point of being sacrificed; the time of my departure has come. I have fought the good fight, I have finished the race, I have kept the faith [2 Tim. 4:6–7]."

This chapter has followed the testimony of Paul found in his letters. He had seen the risen Lord, but he never claims authority through ordination. His claim is that of authentic experience with the risen and living Lord Jesus. This priestly authority is more like that of Melchizedek in Genesis 14:17–23 and of Jethro in Exodus 18. The order of Aaron is temporal, but the order of Melchizedek has eternal validity (Hebrews 7). That inclusive view is open today.

CHAPTER 4

The Meaning of Melchizedek for Contemporary Ministry

George H. Tavard

THE IMAGE OF MELCHIZEDEK POSITS A SERIES OF QUES-
tions today in the areas of biblical exegesis, liturgy, and theology: in exegesis because the name of this mysterious king
appears fairly prominently in two passages of the Old Testament (Genesis 14:18-20 and Psalm 110) and in one long passage
of the New (in the Letter to the Hebrews Jesus is called a
priest "after the order of Melchizedek"); in liturgy because a
long tradition, which goes back to the "church fathers," flour-
ished in the Middle Ages and continues to the present in
Catholic literature, ascribes a "priesthood according to the
order of Melchizedek" to those who, through the sacrament of
orders, are enabled to preside at the eucharist; in theology
because such hyperbolic language needs theological interpretation, in that the symbolic or other relationships between the
image of Melchizedek and the reality of Christ, on the one
hand, and the experience of Christian priesthood and minis-

George H. Tavard, S.T.D., is professor of theology, Methodist Theological School in Ohio, Delaware.

try, on the other, are not self-evident. Our age has generally lost touch with the underlying symbolism that would give sense to the biblical comparison between Melchizedek, Christ, and the Christians.

I shall address first Melchizedek in the Old Testament; second, Melchizedek in the Letter to the Hebrews; third, Melchizedek as seen by the Church Fathers; and fourth, Melchizedek as seen by Calvin, which will lead, by way of contrast, to an ecumenical conclusion.

The Old Testament

The verses in Genesis 14:18-20 bring us little light. On the way back from a victory in battle, Abram is met by Melchizedek. In the normal manner of oriental sovereigns, Melchizedek is both king and priest; more exactly, he is the high priest of the God venerated in his kingdom. The "king of Salem" (whether this is Jerusalem or Salem is a moot point) was "priest of God Most High" *(El Elyon)*. He brought bread and wine in what must have been intended as a ritual gesture, blessed Abram in God's name, and blessed God for giving the victory. In return Abram offered him the tithe of his goods, which I take to mean the spoils of war that his party was carrying back.

Melchizedek reappears in Psalm 110. Here, in a short messianic psalm, Yahweh enthrones the Messiah in his function, making him king and priest: king in Zion (the hill of Jerusalem) and "priest for ever, after the order of Melchizedek." It is appropriate to note at this point that later Judaism entertained speculation about Melchizedek. One finds traces of this in several targumim, in Philo, in Josephus, and in the Qumran literature (11 Q.). In the Christian era Melchizedek appears again in the Book of the Secrets of Enoch. The main point here lies not in the details of the speculation, but in the reference itself: it shows that a properly Christian adoption of

Melchizedek as a sort of spiritual ancestor of Christ could not have been, in its time, as farfetched as it may seem to us twenty centuries later.

The Letter to the Hebrews

Melchizedek occupies a major place in the Letter to the Hebrews in that his name and his symbolism are used as a key to justify and explain the priesthood of Christ.[1] Christ is presented, early in the epistle, as the high priest who brings about the forgiveness of sins (2:17), as the "apostle and high priest" of those who believe (3:1). Just as those who now believe are set apart from those of the old faith, their high priesthood is different from the old one. In fact, Christ, now proclaimed the high priest although he is not of the tribe of Levi, was not a priest in the eyes of the Law. The Law recognized only priests in the line of Aaron, who were easily identifiable by their membership in the tribe of Levi. The epistle does acknowledge, in 5:4, the priesthood of Aaron. This was a legitimate priesthood, in that it was not self-made, but called by God. Like Aaron, Christ was called to become the high priest. But this had to be a different kind of priesthood, identified by the author, with the help of Psalm 110, as the priesthood according to the order of Melchizedek.

The trend of thought of the epistle relative to the symbolic relationship between Melchizedek and Christ is easily discerned. Having identified Jesus as both apostle and high priest, the epistle explains what Jesus does in each capacity. As apostle, that is, messenger, Jesus speaks and spreads the good news. He is the object of the testimony of the Holy Spirit (3:7) to the effect that one should listen to his voice in order to "enter into his rest," which is the rest of the Sabbath. He is the Word of God, living, powerful, "sharper than any two-edged sword [4:12]."

As high priest, "Jesus, the Son of God," has entered the heavens. He was called by God. He prayed during his earthly life and was listened to. He "learned obedience through what he suffered" and was made the "source of eternal salvation" for those who obey him (6:8, 9). A long parenthesis (5:11 to 6:10) encourages the believers to obey and understand, on the basis of their baptismal enlightenment and of God's promise and on the model of the earth (6:7-9), when it receives the rain and bears good fruits, and of Abraham (6:13-17), who persevered and saw the realization of the promise. Those who persevere in hope already pass "behind the curtain" in the wake of Jesus, who has "become a high priest for ever, after the order of Melchizedek." The image of Melchizedek recurs again, precisely at the point where the heavenly destiny and the eternal dimension of hope are evoked as integrally belonging to the disciples of Jesus.

The next major pericope of the epistle analyzes at length the image of Melchizedek, presented as the key to the high priesthood of Christ. This takes the form of a midrash, a parabolic commentary, first, on the Melchizedek of Genesis in his meeting with Abram, and, second, on the Melchizedek of Psalm 110 as the model of the messianic priesthood. The name of Melchizedek is translated "king of justice" and that of his kingdom as meaning "peace." Melchizedek is thus king of justice and peace. The silence of Genesis as to his origins is taken to imply that he had none, a person "without father or mother or genealogy, and has neither beginning of days nor end of life [7:5]." This sets him apart from earthly kings, who, usually owing their kingship to their ancestors' nobility, proudly boast of their genealogy. This is the primary point, which, in the reasoning of the author of Hebrews, "assimilates" him to the Son of God. This was also the occasion for some of the wildest speculation, which presents Melchizedek as a previous incarnation of the Word of God.[2]

A secondary aspect of the personage derives from the ritual action that he performed: Melchizedek blessed Abram, a gesture that can only be made by a superior in favor of an inferior; and Abram paid him the tithe, which is the act of an inferior before his superior. This paying of the tithe brings into the argument the Aaronic priesthood of the tribe of Levi. For, in keeping with the medical science of the period, Levi and his descendants were considered to be incorporated in their ancestor Abram, and thus could be seen as having participated in his paying of the tithe. In paying the tithe the priesthood of the Old Covenant witnessed to the superiority of Melchizedek as a figure and forerunner of the messianic high priest. This leads the author of the Letter to the Hebrews to conclude that the messianic high priest was not to belong to the tribe of Levi (in other words, he was not to be a priest of the Old Covenant), but his priesthood, totally new in relation to that of Aaron, would be modeled on that of Melchizedek. It owes nothing to human ancestry, but everything to God's call. At this point the testimony of Psalm 110 reinforces the argument. For it is to the Messiah that the words are addressed: "You are a priest for ever, after the order of Melchizedek." The author concludes further that the priesthood of Aaron has been abolished and with it the Law. God intervened with an oath in favor of the new priesthood, something God had never done in favor of the Aaronic priesthood.

An additional argument is drawn from the fact that the Levites were many, which was necessary, since each one was bound to die. The new high priest, in contrast, remains unique, for he never dies; he is a priest for eternity. Moreover, the priests of the Old Covenant were themselves sinners, who had to offer sacrifices in atonement for their sins before offering them for the people. The new high priest, however, is sinless. Hence the superiority of the New Covenant: its high priest "has arrived to perfect fulfillment" (see Hebrews 9:28).

From here on the contrast between the two priesthoods is illustrated by the structure of the tabernacle (Exodus 26 and 36) as opposed to the sanctuary in heaven and by some details of the old liturgy, in which priests entered the Holy Place (the Court of Priests in the temple) every day, the high priest alone entering the Holy of Holies, and this once a year, for the Day of Atonement (Leviticus 16:29-34). All this, however, was pre-liminary. With its elaborate rules and ceremonies, the old liturgy was like a *Holy* in relation to the true Holy of Holies in heaven that our high priest has entered. Further, the old high priest brought with him the blood of animals offered in sacrifice, like Moses, who sprinkled the book and the people with blood. But the new high priest has brought his own blood into the sanctuary in heaven. This is the true sacrifice, the only one, offered "at the end of the times" for the sins of all the people.

As a result of his eternal priesthood, Christ, the high priest of the New Covenant, who has offered once for all the only sacrifice acceptable to God (Hebrews 9:11–12), is now in heaven, *sitting* at the right hand of God, unlike the Levitical priests, who have to *stand* by the altar day after day. This admittedly complex demonstration and the conclusions it leads to are summed up in what must be regarded as the central statement of the epistle: "This is a capital point of what we say: that we do have such a high priest, who has taken his seat at the right hand of the throne of the Majesty in the heavens, the minister of the holy places and of the true Tabernacle, which was built by the Lord, not by man" (see Hebrews 8:1–2).

The Letter to the Hebrews offers an original Christology. The accent placed on the nature of Christ's sacrifice in entering heaven after a life of obedience and the shedding of his blood brings together, so to say, aspects of the theology of Paul and the Gospel accounts of the life of Jesus. The most original point lies in linking the unique efficacy of Christ's sacrifice with his entrance once for all into the tabernacle set in heaven. Christ's sacrifice is consummated neither on the cross nor at the resurrection, but in his return into the heavens. This has no parallel in the New Testament. Admittedly, the book of Revelation also describes heaven in the form of a sanctuary; but this is no longer the tabernacle, for it is the podium of a Roman public basilica, itself similar to the shape of a Roman theater. The Apocalypse shows heaven and its liturgy on the model of what the early Christians celebrated. Hebrews, however, sees it not on the pattern of the temple, which presumably has already been destroyed (I regard Hebrews as composed around A.D. 75 and probably addressed to a Jewish community in Rome), but on the pattern of the tabernacle, at the ideal time before the first temple was built.

The Meaning in Context

The texture of the Letter to the Hebrews is made of three intermeshing concerns. First, the community in which or for which the epistle was composed has not yet severed all ties with the cult of the temple. It still looks to the Aaronic priesthood, and especially to the high priesthood at the head of it, as proper models, perhaps even as regretted leaders, for the Christians. It is still impressed by the grandiose ceremonies of the Day of Atonement (Yom Kippur), for which the Sunday morning gatherings of believers for a holy meal, a eucharistic memorial, and the singing of a few hymns can be no match.

For this reason several scholars have suggested that the epistle was addressed to a community that was made up chiefly of priests and Levites, who, having come to believe that Jesus was indeed the expected Messiah, nonetheless regretted their past involvement in the liturgies of the temple, their position of spiritual leadership in the Jewish community, and the general respect in which, as members of the tribe of Levi, they had been officially held. The organization of the Christian *Ecclesia* in the making had no room for privileges owing to ancestry. Indeed, among the Christians who remained in Jerusalem and its neighborhood before the revolt of A.D. 132 and the destruction of the city, the position of authority was held, not by converted priests and Levites, but by relatives of Jesus. These belonged to the amorphous group called, when the Gospels were written, the "brothers of

70

Jesus"; they were presumably, like him, of the tribe of Judah and the line of David. If it is true that many of the priestly families in Jerusalem had been of the party of the Sadducees[3]—over against that of the Pharisees, who, by placing their legal scholarship at the service of the synagogues, were unwittingly preparing the survival of Judaism after the dispersion that was to follow the destruction of the city—then there is a reason for the epistle's insistence on the eternity of the priesthood of Christ. The Sadducees denied the resurrection of the flesh, but the spiritual high priesthood of the one who has entered the heavens with his followers implies his resurrection and theirs.

An alternative suggestion would be that the community in question, being composed of ordinary Jewish Christians (a mix of Diaspora Jews and Palestinian Jewry recently emigrated from Palestine), may have been under pressure by some converted priests and Levites to entrust their leadership to them in order to preserve the continuity of Christian ministry with the Aaronic priesthood.[4] At any rate, in the context of the doctrines and discussions of Hebrews, one may sense a major interest in the structure of the community. We are at a time and in a place of transition, before the pattern of government by presbyters and *episcopoi* had clearly emerged and gradually imposed itself in the diverse colonies of Christian believers.

Second, the author of Hebrews is especially concerned about the notion and practice of sacrifice. The sacrifices of the temple had consisted of killing various animals as an act of renunciation on the part of their owners and of homage to God the Creator. This was the central task of the Aaronic priests. Here, precisely, the image of Melchizedek comes to the fore. For the ritual performed by this king of justice and peace in his blessing of Abram included no shedding of blood. He brought "bread and wine." On the Christian side, the eucharistic memorial, whatever shape it may have taken in the Hebrews community, is the point of reference for the ritual of

71

Melchizedek. The eucharist entitles one to see Melchizedek's bread and wine as a substitute for sacrifices. Admittedly, in the Letter to the Hebrews, Christ has offered himself and shed his blood, which he has brought with him into the heavenly sanctuary. But the point is that Jesus' sacrifice does not lie in the shedding of his blood, but in entering heaven like a Holy of Holies and celebrating there the new Day of Atonement. The Greek term *dia*, usually translated as "through" (9:12) (i.e., through his blood, not through that of animals), ought to be read with the sense of "across": the Levitic high priest entered the Holy of Holies by walking, as it were, across the blood of an animal that he had just slaughtered. But Jesus has entered the heavens by walking across his own blood, shed neither by himself nor by any legitimate priest, but by the disbelief of priests and Levites and the mistrial that had taken place before the great Sabbath of Passover.

I understand this point along the lines of Rene Girard's proposal that the chief contribution of Jesus and the early Christians to the religions of humankind was that they did away with the old and apparently universal idea that the shedding of blood is pleasing to God, that in order to be acceptable to the Creator it is appropriate to kill some creaturely being chosen for that purpose.[5] This is, one should admit, a peculiar notion. If, prescinding from the religious traditions and doctrines of most of humanity, one is able to look at the matter without prejudice, one can see only an anomaly in the idea of sacrificial offering to God when this involves the killing of the innocent, as for instance, of twins, a child, a beautiful girl, a slave, a war prisoner, a volunteer, or simply an animal (to mention a few of the sacrificial practices of various religions). Girard, in his anthropological researches, traces such a bizarre practice to some event at the origin of humanity, when the ones who were already or soon to be samples of homo sapiens discovered that the unity of a group in which dissent has arisen can be easily reestablished by banding together against a common victim. Violence became the source of sacred rituals when the collective murder that united its perpetrators gave way to sacrifices of victims, human or animal, to God as the protector and restorer of the threatened unity of a human group. It is not necessary to accept all the details of Girard's theory on the origins of the sacred to agree with his view that the sacrificial notion of the relationships between humanity and God is a strange aberration, for holiness would then be based on injustice and violence. Religious conceptions and theological symbols must be revised in the light of this belated recognition. As the prophets of Israel repeated time and again, what God wants is not sacrifices of bulls and sheep, but the sacrifice of the heart (Isaiah 1:11; Jeremiah 6:20; Ezekial 20:22; Hosea 6:6). Girard reads the Christian message and sees the early image of Jesus Christ in the light of the abolition of sacrificial murder and ritual violence. The death of Christ could not have been a real sacrifice in any sense. In fact, perhaps for the first time in human history, the violence, which led to his crucifixion, brought about no unity. The death of Christ did not function as the ritual killing of a victim usually did and was expected to: despite the opinion attributed to the high priest in John 18:13, the people, instead of being united by the death of its victim, was further divided and soon to be dispersed throughout the world of Rome and Persia. In an ironic allusion to this breaking of the old pattern of violence, Luke noted (in 23:12) that Herod and Pilate, hitherto enemies, became friends; the people was further frustrated of its expected unity by the new friendship between its two tyrants. Again, the separation between the early Christians and the temple·and its cult can well be read in this perspective: ritual violence was renounced, in the knowledge that the violence that caused the death of Jesus was unholy.

In this case, however, the transition cannot have been without turmoil for those among the new believers who had been steeped in the priestly tradition of sacred violence. An important moment in the debate between Gentile and Jewish Christians was constituted by the conflict between Paul and the partisans of James, as this is alluded to in the letters of Paul and in Luke's Acts of the Apostles. The Letter to the Hebrews illustrates a later moment in the inner Christian debate, when both continuity and discontinuity were claimed for the relationship of the new cult to the old. The continuity lies in that both priesthoods were called by God. The much greater discontinuity lies in the abolition of the priesthood of Aaron, now replaced by that of Jesus Christ in heaven, where no sacrifices can be offered other than the eternal offering of the blood of Jesus, whose legal murder, however, had been neither a sacrifice of the temple nor one of the new priesthood, which did not yet exist.

The originality of the new cult in the earliest communities lay in replacing sacrifices with an offering of bread and wine in thanksgiving to God the Creator through the only mediator, Jesus. The inauguration of this offering was attributed to Jesus before he was arrested, tried, and condemned. And, as appears in the theology of Paul, the bread and the wine were identified with the body and the blood of Christ as—in the vocabulary of Hebrews—they have now entered the Holy of Holies.

This is the precise focus for the theology of Hebrews: the introduction of Melchizedek as a priest who must have been higher than Aaron and Levi, since Abram paid him the tithe, entailed the radical suggestion that not only was the Levitical priesthood now abolished, but furthermore, it had been only an anomalous, if perduring, element in the relations between Israel and God. The sacrifices enjoined by the Law were, according to Hebrews 8:5, not even offered to God, but only to "an image and a shadow of the heavenly realities." One could hardly imagine a more thorough indictment of the Levitical priesthood and the cult of the temple, since the first commandment of the Law forbade the making of images of God and of heavenly realities. The Mosaic ordering of the tabernacle, built "on the model that had been shown on the mountain," had been extended to the very object of the cult: this is not God, but an image and shadow.

The real antecedent for Christ's priesthood was that of Melchizedek, which had existed long before God's choice of Aaron and the later designation of the tribe of Levi as holding the Aaronic priesthood. To what extent the community of Hebrews centered its worship on a eucharistic memorial may be debatable, although the reference to Melchizedek implies an allusion to an offering of bread and wine, even if this is not explicitly stated. Yet, in the absence of an explicit mention, the eucharist as such cannot have been prominent in its community.

Third, an additional concern in Hebrews follows on the issue of sacrifice. If, as it seems, the author removes the Christian worship (in the strict sense of liturgical sacrifice) to heaven, then the most important factor in the life of Christian believers is not ritual, but spiritual. Faith is the central focus of common prayer in official rites. This may be covered briefly, since it is not directly tied to the image of Melchizedek. Yet it may be of major import for our own conclusion. The relation of the faithful to Christ as the only high priest of the New Covenant, the only mediator, is by faith. In the subtle move, perhaps destined to win over those who still held the old priesthood in high regard, the author claims for faith many of the saints who lived under the Old Covenant: they form "a great cloud of witnesses." What counts in the life of the believing community, whether under the Old or the New Covenant, is not sacrifice, temple, or sanctuary: it is faith, "the assurance of things hoped for, the conviction of things not seen [11:1]." This thread bound the saints together as they succeeded one another in the history that is summed up in Hebrews 11. It was also the warp and woof of life with God. This was already true amoung "the ancients" and it remains so today. But there is a New Covenant; faith is also new: it is now mediated by Jesus Christ, who is no longer an object of hope and desire envisaged in the future, but a present living Person. The ancients were looking forward to the fulfillment of the promises made to Abraham; the faithful look forward to a fulfillment, but their hope is based on faith that the Lord has come. Christians already share in the fulfillment, since they already have access "to Mount Zion and to the city of the living God, the heavenly Jerusalem, and to innumerable angels in festal gathering, and to the assembly of the first-born who are enrolled in heaven, and to a judge who is God of all, and to the spirits of just men made perfect, and to Jesus, the mediator of a new covenant, and to the sprinkled blood that speaks more graciously than the blood of Abel [12:23–24]." In the light of this faith the last chapters of the epistle paradoxically interpret the death of Jesus on the model of the old sacrifices: Jesus "suffered outside the gate" (13:12), just as the burnt offering took place "outside the camp" at the remote time before the first temple was built. Yet even then it is not said that "the sanctification of the people through his blood" was a sacrifice. On the contrary, this symbolism suggests the proper attitude of discipleship: "Let us go forth to him [Christ] outside the camp [13:13]." As to liturgy, that of Christ is in heaven and that of Christians is, on earth, "a sacrifice of praise to God, that is, the fruit of lips that acknowledge his name [13:15]."

Augustine's Interpretation

A funny thing happened to Melchizedek on the way to the twentieth century. Beginning in the third century the theologians of North Africa reinterpreted the symbolism of Hebrews. Cyprian of Carthage first, and then Augustine of Hippo, exploited the image of Melchizedek in a new direction that was certainly not that of the biblical author.[6]

Cyprian was the first among the Church Fathers to see the priesthood of Melchizedek as eucharistic; and the eucharist was, for him, sacrificial, because it was the offering of the sacrifice of Christ. In his Letter 63 to Cecilius, another bishop, Cyprian argued against holding eucharistic celebrations without wine, with water only in the cup. This is against the principle of doing what Christ did at the Last Supper. Cyprian built an argument on Noah being drunk with wine, not with water. He also saw "the sacrament of the Lord's sacrifice" as "prefigured in the priest Melchizedek," who was "a type of Christ." Psalm 110 was introduced. The "order of Melchizedek" was defined as "that which comes and descends from Melchizedek being a priest of God Most High, offering bread and wine, blessing Abraham." Cyprian then asked: "Who is more a priest of God Most High than our Lord Jesus Christ, who offered sacrifice to God the Father, and offered him the same thing that Melchizedek had offered, bread and wine, namely, his body and blood?" In this theology the sacrifice of Christ and that of the church are one: "The passion is the sacrifice that we offer." This sacrifice was prefigured by Melchizedek.

Augustine, toward the end of the *City of God*, alludes briefly to the order of Melchizedek as that in which Christ was a priest. He has just explained the eschatological reign of "the priests of God and of Christ for a thousand years together with Christ" (see Revelation 20:6). At this point it is not the millennium that draws his attention: he has refuted literal millenarianism (the theory that Christ will reign with the saints for a thousand years) earlier, as in *City of God*, Book XX, chapter 10. Rather, the identity of these "priests of God and of Christ" concerns him. He understands the biblical text, "not indeed of the sole bishops and presbyters, who are properly called, in the church, *sacerdotes*; but, as we are all called christs on account of the mystical christ (used in baptism), so are we all called priests, because we are members of the one priest." The believers' communion in the body of Christ that is the church, their constituting together, in Augustine's language, "the total Christ," makes them priests. As believers share Christ's (mystical) body, they share by the same token his priesthood; all Christians are "priests after the order of Melchizedek." Augustine then concludes that the expression

77

"priests of God and of Christ" means "priests of the Father and the Son," thus suggesting the divine equality of the Son with the Father; yet, "as, due to the form of the servant, he is son of man, so Christ has been made priest for eternity according to the order of Melchizedek." In other words, the humanity of Christ, when it has entered heaven, is raised to an eternal priesthood. Augustine then adds a vague reference to previous passages: "We have spoken of this in this work more than once." Indeed, other texts in the *City of God* speak of Melchizedek, at least by way of brief allusion. The most explicit is in Book XVI, when Augustine, referring to Abraham, explains:

> He was then blessed by Melchisedek, a priest of God Most High; about whom many great things are written in the epistle to the Hebrews, which many say is from Paul, though others deny it. There, for the first time, appeared the sacrifice which is now offered to God by Christians in the whole world, and there, long after the fact, is fulfilled the prophecy addressed to Christ, who then was still in the flesh: You are a priest for eternity according to the order of Melchisedek; not, that is, according to the order of Aaron, which was to disappear at the dawn of the realities announced in these shadows.

Augustine thus introduces Cyprian's idea in his reading of Hebrews: Melchizedek anticipated "the sacrifice" of Christians. Whether Pauline or not (Augustine does not know and apparently does not care), the epistle contains the first mention of the sacrifice offered by Christians. Obviously, Augustine has in mind the eucharist. Yet, on the one hand Hebrews had said nothing explicitly of the eucharist; on the other, it had not equated bread and wine with sacrifice. The only sacrifice that Hebrews speaks of is that of Christ; and, like his priesthood, it is not a phenomenon of earth, but of heaven, even though the blood of this sacrifice was shed on earth at the death of Jesus. Only the entrance of Christ into the heavens retroactively gave a sacrificial dimension to his death. Now, however, in Cyprian's and Augustine's reading, the bread and wine of Melchizedek were shadows thrown into the story of Abraham by the action of the church offering a sacrifice to God. What is this sacrifice? Book X, chapter 6, proposes Augustine's famous definition: "A true sacrifice is every action by virtue of which we may adhere to God, relative to the attainment of that good, thanks to which we may truly be happy."

This Augustinian perspective of the blessed and happy life is, so to say, christianized when, subsequently, in chapter 20, Augustine specifies that Christ is the only mediator of sacrifice: in "the form of God" he receives the sacrifice along with the Father; yet "in the form of the servant he prefers to be the sacrifice rather than to receive it. . . . By this he is the priest, being the offerer and also the offering." Yet Christ did not want to be the only offerer: "He wanted the daily sacrament of this to be the sacrifice of the Church, which, since it is the body of Him who is as the Head, has learnt to offer itself through him." Elsewhere, in Book XVIII, chapter 25, Augustine ties Malachi's prophecy of "a pure offering in every place," with Christ's sacrifice, with Melchizedek, and with the daily sacrifice offered in the church: "This sacrifice we see being offered in every place from the rising to the setting of the sun, through the priesthood of Christ according to the order of Melchizedek."

In this way Augustine has undoubtedly, following Cyprian, distorted the meaning of Hebrews. Where Hebrews had only one sacrifice of the New Covenant, begun indeed on earth in the death of Christ but consummated in heaven where the risen Jesus properly becomes the new high priest, Augustine has daily sacrifices in the church, set also under the aegis of the "order of Melchizedek." Augustine is, at this point, extremely ecclesial. Yet he is not clerical. The priesthood pertains to the people of faith: "Priesthood *(sacerdotium)* signifies here the people itself, the priest of which is the Mediator between God and men, the man Christ Jesus." For this reason Christians are called "holy people, royal priesthood" in the First Letter of Peter. As to the sacrifice, it is Christ: "He is the sacrifice, not according to the order of Aaron, but according to the order of Melchisedek; may those who read, understand [Bk. XVII, ch. 5]." These last words suggest that the matter is more mysterious in Augustine's mind than it looks. In any case the priesthood of the whole people is no answer to the church's need for "priests and Levites":

> Not from flesh and blood, like the first priesthood according to the order of Aaron, but, as it was proper in the new Covenant, in which Christ is the high priest according to the order of Melchisedek, we now see priests and Levites elected according to the merit of each as given to each by divine grace.

The Modern Problem

In his commentaries on Genesis and Hebrews, Calvin duly noticed that, unlike the Church Fathers, the epistle does not argue from the bread and wine of Melchizedek to his similarity with Christ. He concluded that "these Fathers invented a sacrifice of which Moses never thought."[7] Yet he fully endorsed the symbolism of Melchizedek, who had "the figure of Christ printed in him and who is as it were, his representation and correspondence." The bread and wine, however, were only food that the king of Salem, with "royal liberality," placed at the disposal of Abram and his army. The "*ordo* of Melchizedek" becomes "the form of Melchizedek," this being the unity of kingship and priesthood, operative in Melchizedek, forbidden to the kings of Israel and Judah, and restored in Christ, in whom neither office can be separated from the other. Although these statements differ considerably from those of the Church Fathers, Calvin's method of interpretation is not unlike theirs.

The Fathers of North Africa invested the symbol of Melchizedek in Hebrews and, by implication, in Psalm 110 and Genesis, with the richness of their own experience and theology of the eucharist. This was not unlike what the author of Hebrews had himself done when he invested the Melchizedek of Psalm 110 and Genesis with the wealth of his own experience and theology of Christ.[8] Likewise, Calvin invests the Melchizedek of Hebrews and the Old Testament with his own theology of the functions of Christ. The symbols of the Old Testament were not read forward, from the Old to the New, but backward, from the New to the Old. The meaning of the symbol is then entirely dependent on what one takes it to be, in technical terms, the antitype of the type discovered in the older scripture. No one, by simply reading Genesis or even Psalm 110, would ever arrive at a knowledge of Christ or the eucharist. By projecting back into the Old Testament the experience of the New (as was done by the author of Hebrews) and, further, by projecting back into the New Testament the experience of the church in one's time (as was done by the North African Fathers), one gives new meaning, unknown to the original author, to a text. This is not in keeping with a strictly historical approach to scripture, but it is in accord with a symbolic reading of texts. A text exists as soon as it is available to readers, who read it symbolically by recognizing in it elements of their experience.

One could learn from this that contemporary approaches to biblical literature are in danger of considerably impoverishing our reading of the word of God: the word is not the nude text; it is the text as meaning-ful, as invested with the wealth of experience of the subsequent Christian community. The problem of symbolic reading is one of discernment: how can one choose the proper referent, the "prime analogue," in the light of which "analogies" can be found in older texts? These may be called "anticipations," provided one remember that, like prophecies that are known as prophecies only through their fulfillment, the anticipations are placed in the text afterward, by our reading. The symbolic principle for Christian reading of the Old Testament is the New: Christ is the key to all that came before. This process was at work in the New Testament itself, not least in the writings of Paul. Cyprian and

81

Augustine implicitly concluded from this that the symbolic principle for reading the New Testament is the contemporary Christian experience. Catholics have always been at home with this principle, even if they have at times abused it. Protestants have generally been uncomfortable with it, sometimes because, like Calvin, they disapproved of the contemporary referent; sometimes perhaps, although I have not found this articulated in Luther's or Calvin's comments,[9] because they did not see how it fits the principle of the primacy of scripture. Is the Christian community then simply, before the image of Melchizedek, at a classic point of divergence between Catholics and Protestants? Were this the case, Melchizedek would be an invisible and silent participant, watching with interest and a bit of irony over the current ecumenical dialogues about eucharist, ministry, and priesthood: both sides, in the past, claimed him; both sides, today, ignore him.

It is good to end an essay on a reverent affirmation of the need for holiness in ministers. But it probably does not help much. Even if one believes in the possibility, by the grace of God, of searching for and perhaps reaching perfection here on earth, neither holiness nor perfection depends on what we do. Can the meditation on the image of Melchizedek lead us to more practical conclusions for ministry today?

It all depends on whether the largely forgotten Melchizedek can be seen again as meaningful in the contemporary context. In my book *A Theology for Ministry*[10] I analyzed the four lines along which Christian ministers have functioned. I called them mediation, proclamation, service, and education. And I suggested that only the first requires ordination; the other three, although structurally tied to the first in theory as in practice, being properly performed by all the baptized members of the Christian community. In the language that, whether one likes it or not, has become traditional, only the first, mediation, is a priestly function in the sense of the Latin *sacerdos* and the Greek *hierateuma*. The theory is of course that the risen Christ, the sole high priest of

82

the New Covenant, can and does associate to his priestly function, by the operation of the Holy Spirit, the members of the church: first, all the faithful, through faith and baptism, are chosen to offer God the spiritual sacrifice of a devoted life; and then, through ordination and orders, a smaller number of believers are so called and empowered that they may be recognized as properly leading the community in the great eucharistic prayer.

A new sense of symbols is needed in the ministry of all the Christian churches today. The mark of the Creator remains impacted in this universe. The realities of the world, in their materiality and the richness of the complex experience that they offer, are themselves filled with the Creator's grace. A new discernment of this ought to lead to a further perception of Jesus, the Christ, the Logos made flesh, as the Word specifically spoken to humanity both through and above the symbolism of creation. The symbol of Melchizedek, as reinterpreted in the Letter to the Hebrews, presents one of those few points where the options are clear for a reconceptualization of ministry: either the image of Melchizedek is totally irrelevant because Christ is not the high priest to whom the image points, who abolished the sacredness of violence, and therefore can be followed only in love and surrender; or the symbol of Melchizedek highlights the reality of the true king of justice from whom we receive, as Abram from the king of Salem, the call to take part in his offering of bread and wine, the most ordinary food of human civilization having been transformed into a rite of entrance into the kingdom of God. In simpler terms, contemporary ministry ought to focus not on what can be done with techniques and achievements, but on what Christ does in us and through the church in the eucharist.

Implications for Ministry

What can this imply for the practice of Christian ministry today? Admittedly, the scriptures do not provide detailed solutions to the contingent questions and problems that arise at specific periods of history. This is as true today as it was in the past. Furthermore, it is not the task of theologians to tell ministers what to do in their daily care of souls. Yet a few suggestions, which are by no means exhaustive, may be made in the light of the preceding reflection on the symbolism of Melchizedek in the Letter to the Hebrews.

First, the image of Melchizedek as a symbol of the high priesthood of the risen Lord should provide ministers with meaningful points of reference for self-understanding and continuing spiritual formation. Christ alone, in his risen humanity, is the mediator of the New Covenant; therefore, ministers should act as messengers of the High Priest in heaven, not interpose their personal ideas and idiosyncracies between the people and the risen Christ.

Through modern technologies, contemporary life is exposed to an abundance of secular images that often implicitly suggest a practical agnosticism, or even atheism. This second image of Melchizedek should help ministers and their congregations recover a deeper sense of the importance of religious symbols. Although the great Reformers commented on the Letter to the Hebrews, Protestant preaching in more recent times has neglected this letter. It has preferred the great Pauline writings, especially the Letter to the Romans, because these are more clearly focused on justification by faith. Catholic preaching, on the contrary, has continued to use the Letter to the Hebrews largely because sacerdotal or priestly language has remained frequent in Catholic catechesis and teaching and is still familiar to the people. In our ecumenical age, however, the Catholic use of the symbol of Melchizedek should no longer inspire a Protestant mistrust of this image, which evokes the heavenly life and points to the substance of the Christian hope in a secular world.

Third, the symbol of Melchizedek can help modern piety and devotion to pass from what has been called a "Jesusology" to an authentic Christology. Jesusology designates a form of

Christian piety in which the memory of the human Jesus predominates. Westerners like to imagine this human Jesus on their own model and have become familiar with the popular picture of Jesus as a blond, long-haired, bearded, soft-looking, and slightly absent-minded European. By contrast, this has provoked black theology to see him as black and some feminist theologians to present "him/her" as a female. A Christocentric piety, on the contrary, is focused on the universal elements in the salvific function of Christ. As the high priest according to the order of Melchizedek, the mediator of Christian faith and piety is now in heaven, where there is "neither Jew nor Greek , . . . neither male nor female [Gal. 3:28]." Christ's risen humanity has passed beyond distinctions of race and sex.

Finally, the image of Melchizedek may help restore the Christian liturgy to its rightful place and proper structure. In particular, it can contribute to a new sense of the Trinitarian form of prayer and especially of the eucharistic prayer. For the eternal High Priest is no other than the Word of God and, in traditional language, the Second Person of the Holy Trinity. This may give deeper meaning to the principle that Christians pray *to* God, *through* the Word, and *in* the Holy Spirit.

CHAPTER 5

Antique Clothes and a Digital Watch: Ordination, Why, Who, and For What?

Constance F. Parvey

For a course on American religious traditions, students were required to visit a worship service of their choice and report their experiences to the class. One young man, a religious inquirer who belonged to no religious community, went to a Roman Catholic Mass at a nearby church. "The congregation sang a lot," he said, "and everyone ate some sort of thin wafer; the man at the center who talked and distributed the wafers was dressed in antique clothes and wore a digital watch." This student made the astute observation that antique clothes and digital watches were incongruous with each other. Although not raised in the Christian church, he captured the contradiction between the unconscious ways we accept major social and technological changes and at the same time hold on to what seems to be an "unchangeable" past.

Since the 1960s issues of ministry and ordination have re-

Constance F. Parvey, B.D., teaches theology at the Lutheran Theological Seminary in Philadelphia.

ceived intensive focus in both Roman Catholic and Protestant churches, but for widely differing reasons. The Roman Catholic Church has a shortage of priests and yet a growing, vigorous movement in Latin America and in Europe for "base communities," or house churches. In the United States, Womanchurch is a similar, self-identified community of nuns and laywomen. In contrast, Protestant churches have an oversupply of priests/ministers. With shrinking parishes and too few in the pew, there are expanding expectations of what the priest's/minister's and church's role ought to be in the changing life-contexts of suburbs, exurbs, and urban areas and in mission at home and abroad. One Presbyterian pastor described the insecurities of her new role in the following words:

> I had been in my office no more than an hour on my first day of work when I received word of a serious automobile accident that had put a church member in intensive care. During the next few weeks I faced countless new pastoral situations each of which carried its own share of human suffering. However caring a person may have been before becoming a pastor, chances are she or he has never before faced so many people in need. It is only natural that we experience doubts: Can I really do this job?
>
> Many other factors intensify the insecurity of the new pastor. For example, church members have come to assume that the pastor will serve as the church's figurehead. They expect a certain demeanor and style of dress; they look forward to various ceremonial appearances of the pastor. But they usually cannot articulate these expectations. The new pastor realizes that the people are expecting many things, but she is not told exactly what.[1]

Contemporary theologians have given much attention to the theological and pastoral problems of ministry in modern society. Prominent among them are Karl Rahner, Edward Schillebeeckx, George Tavard, Rosemary Ruether, and Hans Kung.[2] Likewise, the World Council of Churches, through its Faith and Order Commission, has been working in this area for twenty years.[3] Among the questions explored are the following: (a) celibacy: is it a necessary requirement for ordained ministry? (b) gender: do you have to be male to be a priest? (c) priesthood: is service to, with, and for the people the prime mark of priesthood, or is it sacrifice, with the priest as representative functionary of Christ in the liturgy to the people? (d) homosexuality: should sexually active homosexual persons be ordained? (e) mission: what is the relationship of the church to humanity in a divided and changing world? (f) cultural pluralism: how much indigenization and diversity can there be in both the theory and the practice of ordained ministry? (g) authority: does power come from below, from the people, or from above, the hierarchy (many of whom are not elected, but appointed)? (h) pastoral experience: are the needs of people in present contexts, as determined by empirical evidence, more important than preserving Apostolic Tradition? Underlying each question is the larger issue: What is the church? And indeed what do we Protestants and Catholics mean when we talk about the church and the ordained ministry, and how do church and minister relate to each other?[4]

Barbara Brown Zikmund, dean of the Pacific School of Religion, writes about the church in the United States today as she understands it anew in light of the impact made on her by the World Council of Churches' Sixth Assembly in Vancouver (1983).

How difficult it is for people to value religion in the North American context. Indeed, we live in a society where religion does not have the central importance and power it once enjoyed. People may still attend church and speak generally about God and country, but theological seriousness is rare. The Christian religiosity that dominated American history for over two hundred years no longer exists. We live in a secular society. Today, the so-called mainline churches are far from the center of power. In fact, being a Christian in America has become marginal.

This new reality changes my understanding of theology, biblical study, and the ecumenical movement. It means that I have a great deal in common with my Christian sisters and brothers around the world. As a member of the worldwide marginal faith community I am increasingly able to appreciate and more eager to seek ecumenical support.[5]

Because the foundational questions are both ecclesial and ecumenical, they extend far beyond the scope of this chapter. To limit and focus the issues concretely, I will examine the understanding of ordination from the point of view of women. By doing this, some of the questions mentioned earlier will be addressed, but they will be dealt with concretely vis-à-vis the particular contexts of women—the why, who, and whats related to women in ordained ministry. The question of ordination can be approached in many ways. I draw largely on literature written by women, contrasting these writings with the text in the World Council of Churches' Faith and Order document on *Baptism, Eucharist, and Ministry* (BEM), now widely circulated among the churches. The preparation of the BEM text was a long process and represents a real convergence, if not consensus, at magisterium levels. There has been no similar worldwide process enabling women to draft convergence texts on how they understand ministry[6]; consequently, I draw on a number of texts to examine and contrast women's understandings, both lay and ordained, of the questions posed in relation to those drafted primarily by representatives of church bodies. Finally, I write from my experience as an ordained Lutheran pastor.

Ordination: Why?

With respect to the "why" of ordained ministry, the crucial issues are (a) role modeling, (b) the meaning of priest/minister as a representative function, and (c) the exercise of authority. Because women have few, if any, role models when they become ordained ministers, many of them look to the New Testament and find their model in Jesus' ministry. Their theological emphasis is not so much on Christ as the Lord of the Church, but on Jesus as the model for ministry. This is seen in the preaching and pastoral emphases of women. Their ministry is one of healing, mission, outreach, education, and reconciliation. Their writings contrast significantly with the BEM document, which emphasizes Christ as Lord of the Church, and therefore the minister/priest as herald, ambassador, representative of Christ to the people. The language of BEM is conceptual and general; the language of women theologians and pastors tends to be practical. It emerges from tangible events in their ministerial experience, expressing how they make sense of these through interpretations of the ministry of Jesus. In seeking a common base at the World Council of Churches' Sheffield Consultation on the Community of Women and Men in the Church, 1981, the participants agreed:

> In our vision, the *style of life* is living together as sisters and brothers in the church, as the family of God (Eph. 2:19): sharing money and resources; creating an atmosphere of learning and solidarity; living the gospel and witnessing in society; standing for justice and compassion. In our vision, the leadership of the church is the model of Jesus Christ, who always entered into dialogue. In our vision, the church community in any part of the world is called to be the salt and light of the society in which it stands.[7]

The ordained minister serves not only as a figurehead or ceremonial person, but also in a representative function, particularly in those churches that stress apostolic succession and eucharistic-centered ministries. For women, the justification for this function is founded not so much on concepts of apostolic succession as "an expression of the continuity of the Church throughout history,"[8] but rather in apostolic presence, which is something continually manifested and celebrated in the eucharist. In other words, for many women the significance of the church's ministry for today is first identified and then it is seen within the perspective of past historical experiments. This means that the concept of representative function is not understood as representing the biologically male Jesus or the male apostles. Rather, at the celebration of the eucharist, the ordained person who presides has a representative function in two senses. First, the celebrant has a symbolic significance as a human representative of the whole people (male and female, rich and poor, black and white, young and old, etc.) and uses signs, gestures, and imagery that are "inclusive" or "whole" to signal this expanded insight into the nature of representative function. Second, the celebrant works to enrich the vision of the eucharistic prayer to include the women apostles named in scripture along with the women teachers, martyrs, saints, and theologians of the church's tradition through the ages. Many of these women, like Mary, Martha, Junia, and Phoebe of the nascent church and Julian of Norwich, Hildegard von Bingen, and Margery Kempe of the Middle Ages, are being discovered anew in our time. Thus the eucharistic prayer can incorporate the tradition of women in present celebrations.[9]

Elisabeth Moltmann-Wendel suggests this approach to the apostolic beginnings of the church and the roles of women. She states:

> Church history begins when a few women set out to pay their last respects to their dead friend Jesus. It begins when, contrary to all reason and all hope, a few women identify themselves with a national traitor and do what they consider to be right, what in their eyes equals quality of life, namely, loving one who has sacrificed his life, never abandoning him as dead. Church history begins when Jesus comes to them, greets them, lets them touch him just as he has touched and restored them in their lives. Church history begins when the women are told to share with the men this experience, this life they now comprehend, this life their hands have touched.[10]

The concept of representative function leads naturally to the issue of the authority of ministry. The exercise of authority in the church has been practiced in hierarchical terms, and in that scheme women have been the recipients of teachings, rather than their interpreters and guides. Added to this is the patriarchal nature of authority. Women respond to this elitism of authority and its gender exclusiveness by emphasizing the formation of processes and structures that support authority-in-community and communities of authority as alternative visions of structures. For women this means exploring those methods of common work, teaching, and decision-making that empower the full participation of the diversity of the gifts of the church in mutuality, reciprocity, and sharing.

This contrasts to the test of BEM, in which it seems that the ordained minister has the gifts and the congregation (the laity) merely respond passively in prayer; the ordained person does not acknowledge or lift up their gifts. The BEM text could be interpreted to say that the community is responsible to the ordained, but the ordained is responsible only to Christ: a three-tiered system with clergy as the middle layer. Although clergy and lay language may continue to be used as designations for specific purposes, in the authority-in-community model of leadership, this distinction would not be central for policy and teaching. The functions of the hierarchical model as a sociological type would become obsolete, an antique remnant from a feudal past.

In the Sheffield Report the exercise of authority is discussed as both a gift and a responsibility:

> Authority has often been defined as "power to enforce obedience." However, we believe that authority is merely the right or claim to exercise power. Sources of authority include the model of Christ according to Scripture and also through tradition. . . . Now women as a part of their Christian duty are being called to claim their authority so that they might assume their full share of responsibility. Genuine authority is exercised, according to this perspective, when its existence is recognized and authenticated as a *gift* to the community. It is therefore both present in the person and willingly received by the community.[11]

If community should become the locus for authority, then the question of how the gospel is to be proclaimed is also seen in another light. The task of ministry is seen not so much as "doing service" and "proclaiming the gospel," but as building up a community that shares the gospel, one that not only gives service, but also receives service and receives the gospel, acknowledging that we are all people-in-relationship through Christ. Women as mothers and teachers have a long tradition in both church and society in education and nurture as a listening/hearing process, or, in the words of Nelle Morton, "a hearing into speech." Morton describes what this means by telling the story of Helen Keller.

> If one can be heard to one's own speech, then the speech would be a new speech and the new speech would be a new experience in the life of the speaker. . . . What an astounding experience that one can learn to speak words without ever hearing but only with having been heard. It is strange that we have never understood before that this is what often happened among women. It is tied up with telling our stories. When Helen Keller out of the darkness of her life reached out her hands under the water pump and struggled to speak a word she had never heard spoken by another living being it was far more than memorizing a new word. "Wah Wah" and again with a great effort "Wah Wah." It was not just a word or a number attached to an object to designate or signify utilitarian purpose. This word was her own experience. This word opened to her the concept of words—the secret of language—of self-identification—of history—of literature—of connectedness to other human beings. Once the concept dawned it was the connectedness with the other—a special other—she immediately sought. Where was that loving ear, that persistent hearing, that had tried and tried again to break through Helen's silence and hear her into this new world of speaking? When she found her teacher, Helen threw herself into her arms, grateful for the profound gift of herself. [12]

A gift that women bring from their past to ministry is these new experiential contexts and thus new methods of proclamation, not from proclaimer to proclaimed-to, but an opening of proclamation through a listening and hearing ministry that uncovers layers of scripture's "good news" in touch with life in its dailiness—with all its sin and grace, its corruptions and glory.

United Methodist woman, Bishop Leontine T. C. Kelly, says of preaching: "The powerful Black preacher recognizes no cleavage between the purpose of the Spirit and the empowerment of a people. . . . The Black woman preacher inherits the authenticity of the Black church and its preaching. She seeks to preserve the warmth, the uninhibited response, the informality, the freedom of the tradition."[13]

Ordination: Who?

The "who" of ministry has expanded in many directions. Since the Middle Ages, Christianity has steadily moved beyond its European origins and shed its imperial attitudes. It has discovered richly different cultures of the world where it is becoming indigenous. In many countries, congregations themselves have become microcosms of "the global village" through changing patterns of migration and technological innovations in communication that make Bishop Desmond Tutu in South Africa a bishop of the church universal, as parish pastor Martin Luther King Jr. was prophet in the United States. Most women who write about *who* should be ordained emphasize words such as wholeness and inclusiveness. They perceive that ordained ministry has become a lopsided pyramid and that preconceived "divinely ordained 'archetypes'" are in need of being tested with respect to (a) their non-theological, societal origins in the past, (b) changing situations today, (c) new aspirations of peoples, and (d) present signs of the reign of God.

Understandings of Christianity also have changed, expanded, and undergone transformations as Christians have emerged in many non-Western societies. In the West, Christians now live, not in feudal structures, but within democratic countries where equality of peoples, women and men, population minorities, and the poor, is supported by law. This means that experientially the "who" of the church's ministry are no longer white, Western, and male, but, as well, of many races, non-Western, and female. We need a positive and inclusive anthropology to express how Christ is concretely at work, transforming the participants in ministry to meet utterly new situations.

To focus on the "who" of ordained ministry opens a basic problem with the ministry section of the BEM text. Its model and norm for ordained ministry is androcentric, male-centered. Because this has been the dominant tradition for hundreds of years, it comes as no surprise. However, a second norm of BEM is that the minister is able-bodied and from only certain racial, class, or ethnic groups. The first norm is obvious in paragraph 18 dealing with "The Ministry of Men and Women in the Church." It begins with a strong biblically based theology of equality using Paul's language of Galatians 3:27-28: "There is in Christ no male or female." However, in describing the gifts of ministry, it states: "Both women and men must discover together their contributions to the service of Christ in the Church." Then it continues: "The Church must discover the ministry which can be provided by women as well as that which can be provided by men."[14] By proposing a gender-based two-track system, this sentence undermines what has just been said. It is an accommodation to those churches that oppose the ordination of women. Although this ecumenical issue is important to address, it is quite another matter for all churches to consent to a gender-differentiated system of ordained ministries, ruled by "biology as destiny," meaning specialized, ascribed women's ministries.

In paragraph 50 of BEM other nonnormative persons are addressed: those who are handicapped and those in other groups. The text implies a rebuke to churches that "refuse" to ordain them; but then it hedges with the much softer word reevaluate. It states: "Churches which refuse to consider candidates for the ordained ministry on the grounds of handicap or because they belong, for example, to one particular race or sociological group should re-evaluate their practices."[15]

It is significant that in this paragraph no positive moral or biblical imperative is drawn on to compel or inspire the churches in the direction of inclusiveness, yet the ministry of Jesus is replete with examples of choosing socially marginalized and "not whole" people as vehicles for divine revelation and signs of the reign of God. In BEM there is basically one androcentric model that is normative for ordained ministry and a peripheral model, or deviation, for women and "others." Women and "others" should not need to "be included"; the larger issue to address is why they continue to be left out and what efforts must be made in order that they can be more fully incorporated.

Una Kroll, a medical doctor and Anglican theologian, writes about the "who" of ordained ministry in an inclusive way:

As a living human being Christ was a man. His sex was part of him: yet it was not his wholeness, and when he died he was freed from its limitations. Sexuality is an important and intimate part of every human being, yet it is not the whole of a person, nor can it be said that God relates only to femaleness or to maleness, or to a precise sexual balance in any one person. The image of God is to be found in heterosexual women and men, but it is also found in homosexuals, trans-sexuals, bisexuals, hermaphrodites and eunuchs. These people are not lacking in humanity because they are not the average. Christians have never found sexuality easy to understand, but to my knowledge, no theologian has ever said that anyone who is a homosexual, a bi-sexual or a trans-sexual by nature is automatically excluded from the "in Christ" relation because of her or his sexual orientation. Their humanity is more important than their sex. In the same way, women as well as men are included in the "in Christ" relation and always have been.[16]

A related issue to the "who" of the ordained ministry is the "call." According to BEM: "People are called in differing ways to the ordained ministry. There is a personal awareness of a call from God to dedicate oneself to the ordained ministry. This call may be discerned through personal prayer and reflection, as well as through suggestion, example, encouragement, guidance coming from family, friends, the congregation, teachers, and other church authorities."[17] Although it is acknowledged that the call comes in many ways, the text states additionally that each person must be "authenticated by the Church's recognition of the gifts and graces of the particular person, both natural and spiritually given." Because the call is a gift of the community and to the community, some process is necessary to ensure that this gift is honored. However, in cases where women receive calls and their churches do not ordain them, the process is frustrated. Fran Ferder, F.S.P.A., has interviewed many Roman Catholic women who have received calls to priesthood. She describes the call of one such person as a "clear, unmistakeable call from God." She develops what this call means:

> To be a priest is to have childhood musings about ministry—in the Temple at age twelve and begin to know that we must be about our creator's business. It is to sense that we have a responsibility for the holy as we see the first water turned into wine. It is to grow more sure of our source as we experience ourselves binding up the wounds of the brokenhearted. To be a priest is to spend lonely nights on mountains, listening, staying in touch with the God who never stops calling. To be a priest is to know, at some point in life, as did Mary Magdalen, that we have to be involved in the banquet, even though we haven't been invited. This woman, this priest, was sure of that. I was sure of it too, the more I talked with her.
>
> As we talked further, I found myself getting caught up in the excitement of her present ministry. It was somewhat confusing. What she felt most called to was denied her. She was frustrated, angry, sad about this. But she did not seem crippled by it. She

was deeply involved in serving, in enabling others. She clearly loved what she was doing now. I wondered what she did with her anger. "I decided a long time ago," she told me, "that I wasn't going to sit back and feel sorry for myself because I couldn't be a priest. I wasn't going to give the present structure that kind of power over me. I wasn't going to let it keep me from serving now."[18]

For ordained women in Protestant churches, the issue is not exclusion, but male preference. Edward C. Lehman Jr., in his study of clergywomen, found that even in local churches that have had an ordained woman on the staff, usually as an assistant or associate, 65 percent of the members preferred a man, particularly as a "senior pastor."[19] If one puts together the two situations of women, Catholic and Protestant, then it is clear that more effort from policymakers must be undertaken to transform the patriarchal attitudes in the churches, held by women and men. If the churches are going to benefit from the "natural and spiritual" gifts of ordained ministry that women and "others" are able to bring to its mission, then it must work to overcome its own internal roadblocks. This means that the "who" of the church is more than a matter of personal call; the church itself must recognize a call to meet these new aspirations and signs.

Ordination: For What?

From the question of "who" is ordained, we move to the question of "for what?" Paragraph 35 of BEM addresses the question by saying that a purpose of ordained ministry is to "serve the proclamation of the apostolic faith."[20] In other places as well, the document underlines the function of proclamation as essential to the nature and vocation of the church itself. "In ordaining, the church . . . provides for the faithful proclamation of the Gospel and humble service in the name of Christ."[21] This means that proclamation and service are seen as essential tasks of the church, and it is the ordained minister who provides them. Once again what is significant in these citations is that these tasks of the church are not seen as reciprocal between the ordained and the laity, but as hierarchical: moving from Christ to the ordained and then to the congregation. This top/down movement of authority is reiterated through the "setting apart" of the ordained.[22] Although the text states that ordination is not a possession of the person, but a "gift for the continual edification of the body in and for which the minister is ordained," the overriding context puts the initiative of "for what" on the ordained rather than on the community. Again it is not reciprocal. This can be seen in paragraph 16, where the community serves the ordained, but not vice versa; it states: "Only when they [the ordained] seek the response and acknowledgement of the community can their authority be protected from the distortions of isolation and domination."[23]

In contrast, Ada Maria Isasi-Diaz, Roman Catholic theologian, makes a plea for empathy as a fundamental quality of ministry, based on a model of ministry-in-community where equality and liberation are the marks that make empathy possible. She writes:

Empathy is the ability of the heart to feel with the other person. It requires that we open ourselves not only at the intellectual level, but especially at the emotional level. To empathize is to risk, because it necessitates our being vulnerable. Empathy does not ask that you feel the way I do, think the way I do, act the way I do. But empathy does demand that we listen with the heart. It is not only a matter of respecting what others say and do, who they are. Empathy asks that you seriously consider that what is true and good for others might well be true and good for you.[24]

The crux of the matter, stated over and over in many ways, always is found in the nature, location, and exercise of authority. Authority-in-community must be acknowledged in more than a negative sense, as in BEM, where it is viewed primarily as a protection against isolation and authoritarianism. BEM still maintains that the ordained holds authority and exercises it *to* cooperate with the laity (not *in corporation with*). In other words, the movement is from A, who has authority and decides if, when, and how to share it with B. In the community of the Body of which Christ is Head, ordained and lay need to be accountable together. The ordained ministry must be seen within the context of the one mission of the church in ministry wherein members in empathy work with and for each other for the sake of the kingdom. Making a point about democratization in ministry, Karl Rahner writes: "The pastor should remain a pastor, but this certainly does not mean that he is to treat his flock as if they really were sheep."[25]

Thus far in this section I have mainly dealt with sociological and psychological implications of "for what." There is, however, a spiritual-ontological dimension of ordained ministry. This is the given character of ordination itself, symbolized in the act of ordination through the invocation of the Holy Spirit and the laying on of hands. The BEM document states that "the ministry of such persons, who since very early times have been ordained, is constitutive for the life and witness of the Church."[26]

What has happened in the text again is that which is essential for the church has become invested as a sign in the ordained. He/she receives the blessing of the Holy Spirit that belongs to the whole community. He/she becomes the sign, meaning that the vision is narrowed, focusing on the ordained rather than on a specific expression of the one ministry. BEM declares: "Ordination is an invocation to God that the new minister be given the power of the Holy Spirit in the new relation which is established between this minister and the local Christian community and, by intention, the Church universal. The otherness of God's initiative, of which the ordained ministry is a sign, is here acknowledged in the act of ordination itself."[27]

An alternative vision for ordained ministry is that the community, the local church, or the authority-in-community at whatever level, is empowered by the Holy Spirit and strengthened for its task through the appointment of ordained ministers. These persons are recognized and spiritually appointed with the responsibility to represent and oversee certain tasks entrusted to them by the community. This would not be "functionalism," a sociological category, but an expression of the validity of ordained ministry, christologically understood, but expressed in concrete terms.

In this model the community would continue to be responsible for its constitutive, Christ-centered, pneumatological tasks expressed not only in the office of ordained ministry as now viewed, but also in other offices and forms of diversified ministries according to the needs of the church, its lay and ordained, paid and unpaid ministers. In this model the ordained ministry would focus on the specific work that they must guarantee on behalf of the community, tasks such as faithfully leading the community in its life of spirituality and prayer, breaking of bread, proclamation, teaching, and service.

This ordering of ordained ministry would put the emphasis on the Body of Christ as a whole and on the ordained one as a participant in a spiritual covenant. The movement in this model would not be from ordained to community or community to ordained in a linear sense, but ordination within community—challenged, inspired, and judged by the Holy Spirit and the Word-in-community. In this formulation the role of the Holy Spirit would become integral to all aspects of the authority, witness, and "being" of the church. It would highlight what BEM states: "The Spirit blows where it wills (John 3:8): the invocation of the Spirit implies the absolute dependence on God for the outcome of the Church's prayer. This means that the Spirit may set new forces in motion and open new possibilities 'far more abundantly than all that we ask or think' (Eph. 3:20)."[28]

Roman Catholic theologian Catherina Halkes makes an assessment of the need for pneumatology in the church. She writes:

> In theology three areas correspond to the three ways in which God reveals himself: the theology of creation, Christology and pneumatology, and of these three pneumatology has clearly been underrated. We simply have to establish a mutually inspiring interaction between these three kinds of revelation. This would bring out the way in which God communicates and would strike the balance between transcendence and immanence. Only in this communicative aspect of the trinity can Christian *anthropology* acquire the significance it deserves.[29]

Early accounts of proclamations of the gospel are found in the Acts of the Apostles; in all cases, it is said that those speaking were inspired by the Holy Spirit. Proclamation and service make sense only when empowered by the Holy Spirit; the church itself and its mission are alive only by the promptings of the descent of the dove. It is this that pushes us to participate more actively in the reign of God than our natural inclinations would want us to go, calling us to the work of transforming those incongruities between antique clothes and a digital watch.

CHAPTER 6

The Priestly Task in Creating Community

William H. Willimon

There is one body and one Spirit, just as you were called to the one hope that belongs to your call, one Lord, one faith, one baptism, one God and Father of us all, who is above all and through all and in all.

—Ephesians 4:4–6

THE FOURTH CHAPTER OF EPHESIANS SETS THE TONE FOR thoughts on the priestly creation of community. Ernst Kasemann notes that Ephesians is probably a collection of liturgical fragments, a panegyric—prayers and hymns mostly baptismal in nature—in which the church becomes the content of theology. The call for "unity in the Spirit [4:3]," probably addressed to conflict between Jewish and Gentile Christians, is the work of the baptismally bestowed Holy Spirit, not merely the outgrowth of some mere *animorum concordia*, a warmhearted fellowship. Community is a gift of the Spirit, not a human achievement; an objective result of the bestowal of

William H. Willimon, S.T.D., is minister to the university and professor of the practice of Christian ministry, Duke University, Durham, North Carolina.

baptism, not of subjective human striving. (In the light of 1 Corinthians 10—12 one wonders why Ephesians 4:5 does not mention the Lord's Supper as well as baptism as a basis for *koinonia*. Probably the other sacrament is assumed.) Nevertheless, it is clear that in this text the gift of the Holy Spirit in baptism is the basis for the creation of Christian community.

From its beginning the Christian church has been deeply concerned with unity, union, community, and communion. A vision so bold as Christ's, a task so great as the one to which he assigned his disciples, a message so powerful as the one he preached can be sustained only by a body of believers who speak and act as one.

In the Acts of the Apostles the Spirit descends on "[people] from every nation under heaven [2:5]." Despite great diversity, each person heard and understood every other person and "all who believed were together and had all things in common [2:44]." Yet one need look no further than the letters of Paul to see that unity, oneness, and communion were more often a goal or an ideal for the New Testament churches, rather than an accurate description of the way things really were: "When you assemble as a church, I hear that there are divisions among you; and I partly believe it," says Paul in 1 Corinthians 11:18.

Unity continues to be a problem for the church. Whether in its worldwide or local embodiment, the church seeks to convert people from all nations, races, ages, sexes, and economic situations, and yet it also seeks to form them into a unified body of believers. It seeks to affirm the unique, God-given diversity of each person and yet to bind that diversity within a cohesive community of faith. It strives to be open to all and yet strives for the intimacy of a close family.

Is it possible for the church to fulfill its mission without thwarting the very unity that it seeks? Unity for unity's sake can be a stifling, artificial straitjacket for the church, a way of avoiding the conflict that may be essential for growth and faithfulness. Perhaps this was what Paul had in mind when he said to the Corinthians, "There must be factions among you in order that those who are genuine among you may be recognized [1 Cor. 11:19]." Even a cursory reading of the New Testament, particularly books like Ephesians, reveals that a major task of early pastors and teachers was the creation of community. In fact, a case could be made that community is *the* reason for the creation of the ordained ministry in the church.

The Role of the Clergy

In rites of ordination the church designates leaders and tells them what they are to do. The statement in the old Lutheran ordinal is typical:

> Ministers of Christ are His ambassadors and as such are to preach the Word and administer the Holy Sacraments. They are appointed to wait upon and serve the Church, . . . to offer before Him the prayers and supplications of His people; to feed, to instruct, to watch over, and to guide the sheep and the lambs of His flock, whom He hath purchased with His own blood.

Luther stated that all baptized Christians share the gifts of the Spirit, the command to preach, evangelize, witness, heal, and serve. This "priesthood of believers" does not mean that each person is his or her own priest, but that each person is his or her neighbor's priest. The First Letter of Peter addresses all the church, not just the clergy, when it says to newly baptized Christians: "But you are a chosen race, a royal priesthood, a holy nation, God's own people, that you may declare the wonderful deeds of him who called you out of darkness into his marvelous light [1 Pet. 2:9]." This is the church's mandate for ministry that all Christians share. Yet, from the earliest stirrings of the church, some Christians were designated for the task of equipping the saints, caring for the church, upbuilding the community, and representing the church as a whole. Ordination puts some Christians under orders, placing on them a responsibility for the structure and health of that community and making them representative community persons: "And his [Christ's] gifts were that some should be apostles, some prophets, some evangelists, some pastors and teachers, to equip the saints for the work of ministry, for building up the body of Christ [Eph. 4:11–12]"; the author of Ephesians was not implying "ordination" in the twentieth-century sense, but recognizing a call to ministry as response to receiving the baptismal charism. Priests, therefore, are a species of a broader genus called ministry. The church has pastors and priests as a function of its mission because certain things need doing in the church.

Ephesians 4:11–12 suggests that certain leadership functions were already well established in the church. The offices are not legitimated, nor are their functions described, except to say that these leaders exist for the equipment of the saints (4:12a). I disagree with those translations that place the comma after "saints" (there is no comma in the original text). I see no implication that these leaders are to assume sole responsibility for "the work of ministry"; all the saints do ministry. The church's priests are priests to the world's priests (the laity). Why? "For the building up the body of Christ [4:12]." The Spirit's gifts, as well as the giftedness of the church's leaders, are directed toward the community qua community.

In his criticism of the medieval priesthood, Luther said that the church sometimes acts as if priests are the only Christians who are called to witness, to serve, to heal. Against medieval definitions of the priesthood, the Reformers asserted that the essence of the clergy is not in some indelible character conferred at ordination. Clergy are "special" because they are community people. They are not some privileged caste set over the lowly laity. The essence of the ordained ministry is essentially relational (whom it serves) and functional (what it does), not ontological (what it is). The priesthood arises from "below," from the church's mundane need for leadership. At the same time it descends from "above," as a gift of the Lord

(Ephesians 4:8–11; 1 Timothy 4:14), a Lord who will not let his people be without the gifts they need to fulfill their mission. The ordained ministry is not a status. It is a function. Ask yourself: What is the difference between a pastor visiting, preaching, baptizing and any other Christian doing these jobs? The essential difference is in the "officialness." When a pastor visits, teaches, preaches, baptizes, the church "reads" his or her actions differently from the same actions done by lay Christians. The pastor bears the burden of tradition, the obligation to represent the whole church through all ages, the responsibility to edify the whole Body, to keep us together in the church. The pastor, like any other Christian, must walk the journey of faith personally. But ordination impels the pastor to walk with the whole church in mind.

The ministries of particular members, whether lay or clergy, can only be understood in the context of the ministry with which the whole church is charged by Christ. A Christian congregation draws its resources for ministry from the congregation's own unified sense of of its purpose and identity. The question is: How is a congregation unified through the priestly tasks? What is the "glue" that holds a diverse collection of Christians together in a unified, functioning, faithful body?

I shall deal primarily with *internal* unifying factors rather than with external ones. Admittedly, so-called *external* factors are major determinants of a congregation's unity—the socio-economic level of a congregation's members, the homogeneity of the surrounding neighborhood, race, age, political views, language, and other shared sociological factors. External factors are primarily "non-theological"; that is, they arise from and depend on circumstances that are neither the creation nor the intention of the Christian faith and its institutions. In recent years the Church Growth Movement has stressed that the surrounding community's homogeneity, coupled with the homogeneity of the congregation, is a key factor in church growth. People are attracted to a congregation whose members are most like them.[1] Although this seems to be an accurate description of the way that social forces help to determine a group's cohesiveness, there is danger in moving from a description of the way things usually are to a prescription for the way things ought to be. This is the danger of the theory and application of the principles of the Church Growth Movement—the questionable move from descriptive to prescriptive.

While acknowledging the pervasive influence of external factors on the unity of a congregation, I limit myself to *internal* factors—those unifying traditions, activities, rites, and symbols within the local church that unify a congregation. First, I isolate and describe those factors, describing them as characteristics that are nearly always present in a unified congregation. Second, I discuss how unity is actually achieved in the day-to-day life of a congregation through certain priestly activities. Finally, I suggest some implications of my findings for contemporary ministry.

Six Requisites for Congregational Unity

There are six requisites for unity within a congregation: Common Identity, Common Authority, Common Memory, Common Vision, Common Shared Life Together, Common Shared Life in the World.[2]

Common Sense of Identity

The congregation must know who it is and to whom it belongs. It must be able to say clearly, "This is who we are and this is who we are not." Those who are outside the congregation should be clearly identifiable. Generally, the greater the degree of difference or "specialness" the congregation's identity carries with it, the greater the degree of unity among its members. For example, early Methodists displayed a high degree of "specialness." They were easily

identified by their social beliefs (abstinence), polity (connec-
tionalism), or worship style ("shouting Methodist" for some,
Anglican vestiges for others). As they lost some of their early
distinguishing characteristics, as they merged with mainline,
mainstream American Protestantism, as they downplayed
their (real or imagined) "specialness" in an effort to participate
in the emerging ecumenical movement, and as mergers took
place within the denomination (1939, 1968), each with its
attendant compromises and adjustments, Methodists went
through a denominational identity crisis. They had moved
from being a sect that, like all sects, had a distinctive identity
to a church that, like all churches, has a more loosely defined
identity.

Lacking a particular theological identity or distinguishing
ethical or political position, many United Methodist congregations now look for other qualities that may be claimed as
special. "First Methodist is concerned about our community,"
its members may say. A congregation's claim of being the
"friendliest church in town" may be confirmed within its own
congregational life. But claims of friendliness, community
outreach, and antiquity, in themselves, do not necessarily
designate a *Christian* church. In fact, the "friendliness" may,
in itself, be a sign that the congregation has lost a claim to a
theological or biblical mark of a Christian church, and therefore seeks its identity elsewhere. Is the "friendliness" that is
offered in the congregation *Christian* friendliness, or only the
same self-affirming amiability of the local country club? How
will the congregation know unless it submits its claims of
specialness and identity to some historic, ecclesial, biblical,
or theological standards of judgment?

Common Authority

The congregation can articulate the gospel by which it is
judged and by which it judges its life together. There must be
some creed, text, person, or constitution, to which the con-

gregation as a whole ultimately appeals in time of internal crisis, something by which behavior and belief are judged, the final arbiter, the ultimate canon, the overall vision. I am speaking here of more than mere bylaws or standard operating procedures. I am speaking of the guiding principles, purposes, and goals that name and guide a congregation, that make the gathering a specifically *Christian* gathering, and that unite the congregation in hope, purpose, and vision with the church universal.

A congregation that suffers from a lack of common authority will find its life together affected in various ways. Without a commonly recognized authority to which everyone can refer and defer, it is difficult to deal constructively with differences of opinion within the congregation. It is impossible to resolve an argument if we cannot appeal to some commonly recognized source or validation for differing points of view. Debate is carefully avoided out of fear that the debate will be divisive rather than productive. The congregation labors to keep everything polite, genteel, and cheerful lest, during a difference of opinion, the group should fall apart because there is no commonly agreed on authority to which differing points of view can appeal.

Contemporary American churches are victims of the same individualism and subjectivity that afflict our culture. Creeds, scripture, liturgy, and tradition are downplayed in an attempt to appeal to purely personal standards of judgment. We find ourselves in a crisis of authority. Congregations that lose the Bible or other historic, creedal statements of faith are forced to seek common authority elsewhere. Authority sometimes resides in the congregation's pastor. Or some lay leader of the congregation will become the commonly recognized authority in matters of belief and practice. Or secular, generalized, culturally defined statements will become normative for the congregation: "It really doesn't matter what any of us believes as long as one is sincere." Or, "Christianity is mostly a matter of what you do rather than what you believe." Unity thus becomes a matter of congeniality rather than a matter of shared faith.

Common Memory

The congregation must have a shared story, a common history through which it understands itself and its mission. Every unified group, if it exists beyond one generation, places great emphasis on its history. The history will begin orally, with charter members recounting for new or younger members "the way things used to be." Early ordeals and struggles, founding fathers and mothers, original buildings and furnishings will be treated with reverence. Heroes will be viewed as models for succeeding generations to emulate. The shared story, the common history gives a congregation its roots, its identity, its authority.

But certain cultural, psychological, political, and even theological factors tend to disrupt, or a least devalue, a congregation's common memory. We Americans have been accused of being "neophyles," lovers of the new. We are a young, adolescent nation in which great concern for the past is often judged to be mere antiquarian or backward-looking conservatism. In the past few years Americans have been deeply impressed by the darker side of their past—slavery, economic victimization, questionable wars. For many Americans the past is the repository of evil rather than virtue. We have found that heroes of the past were often tainted with ideas that we have later judged to be wrong. In such a climate, loving nurture of one's past is suspect.

Within the congregation, a number of factors contribute to a further devaluation of the necessity of common memory. We are a mobile society. In many congregations there is constant influx of new members, accompanied by constant departure of old members. Fewer old-timers are left to tell the congregation's story and few want to hear the story. Newcomers in the congregation are often threatened by old-timers' attempts

111

to recount congregational history, feeling that, since they have not intimately shared in the history, the history excludes them from full congregational participation. The story may be seen as a roadblock to congregational development, a conservative attempt to smother the new wine in decayed wineskins, a source of disunity rather than of unity as the story is used to differentiate between the "newcomers" and the "original members."

Some pastors are threatened by a congregation's common story. The pastor is probably threatened by the story for the same reason that other newcomers may be threatened. The retelling of the congregation's past, the annual celebration of a congregation's "Homecoming" or "Memorial Day" can be a way of telling the pastor, "You are still not really one of us." Could this be why many pastors deliberately devalue or ignore congregational traditions, common memories, yearly celebrations, and cherished patriarchs? The pastor senses that the traditions, celebrations, memories, and matriarchs are a pervasive influence that the pastor does not control.

Common memories become dysfunctional in a congregation's life when they are ignored or transgressed by new members or new pastors. The old-timers react with hostility, rigidity, and entrenchment. Their reaction may arise because the old-timers instinctively sense that if they lose their common story, they will lose something that is part of the basic fabric of the congregation's existence. Common memories should be used rather than abused. Memories can be powerful motivations for behavior. Memory of past events can become a rallying point for creative and adaptive behavior in the present. The writer of Hebrews was using a congregation's memory in this way when he said: "Therefore, since we are surrounded by so great a cloud of witnesses, let us also lay aside every weight, and sin which clings so closely, and let us run with perseverance the race that is set before us, looking to Jesus the pioneer and perfector of our faith [Heb. 12:1–2]."

New members or new pastors in a congregation should

expect a time of formal or informal "instruction" by the old-timers in a congregation's common memories. This is an attempt on the part of the old-timers not only to assert their authority, but also to integrate new members into the life of the congregation. Larger and more transient congregations would be wise intentionally to instruct—through new member's classes, a congregational handbook, congregational sponsors of new members—newcomers in the congregation's common memories.

A congregation's common memory should not be limited to its own particular congregational history. It should encompass the history of the church as a whole. One of the functions of a pastor is to see the large vision, to push a congregation beyond the bounds of the merely parochial—without destroying the particular memory and identity of the particular congregation the pastor serves. When a congregation becomes entrenched in its own local memories and is apathetic and even hostile to the memories it shares with all Christians everywhere, the pastor has a responsibility to expand the congregation's field of memory.

A common memory can be enlarged and, many times, this is a primary task of preaching and worship. Here the story is told, retold, enacted, and celebrated. The Bible is a common memory. The Apostles' Creed is a model for remembering much in a small space. A common memory is most pervasive, most motivating, and most unifying when it is relatively simple and easily transferable from one generation to the next and easily reiterated on a yearly basis. That transference and loving reiteration of a congregation's common memory is a major source of a congregation's unity.

Common Vision

The congregation must share common goals and guides for which it lives and by which it lives. As a common memory identifies where the congregation has been, so a common vision identifies where the congregation hopes to be. There has currently been much stress on goal-setting and planning in the church. The use of goals and objectives to plan the church program and mission can be helpful. So often a congregation sets unrealistic goals for itself, does not adequately define its objectives, and fails to evaluate its work. The goal-setting process can foster congregational consensus and a sense of "ownership" for congregational activities and programs. Goals can help a congregation be specific and realistic in its expectations for the future. Evaluation of the goals at the end of a designated period also can give a congregation a much needed sense of accomplishment.

But defining congregational direction solely in terms of specific, definable, achievable, and measurable goals also can limit a congregation's vision to the operational, the pragmatic, and the reasonable. The Christian vision is inherently "unrealistic" by many of the world's standards. Christian expectations are eschatological, beyond the confines of the present and current programs for human betterment. The priest is more than a mere congregational manager or setter of congregational goals. The priest is a visionary—a dreamer and an interpreter of dreams.

Without common memory and common authority, how will the congregation judge whether or not its goals and vision are Christian? When a congregation lacks a common locus of identity, authority, and memory that is beyond itself and tied to the historic witness of the church, its goals and visions easily become, for example, a 10 percent increase in our budget by the end of the year, a net gain of fifteen new members by the end of our evangelism campaign, a new air conditioning system for the Social Hall. Rather than an increase among people of the love of God and neighbor or the making of disciples for Jesus Christ, the congregation picks visions that seem obtainable within the confines of its own myopic frame of reference. But "where there is no vision, the people perish," said the prophet.

So often we think of worship as an essentially conservative activity. But worship—in which we gather to catch a glimpse of a "new heaven and a new earth," where our eyes are opened in prayer, ecstatic praise (ecstasy means literally "to stand outside oneself"), or eucharistic bread to the presence of God among us—is also a potentially visionary phenomenon, disruptive of the status quo. Unfortunately, it is a sociological fact of life that as a congregation or a denomination matures, its vision blurs. The vision that originally motivated the founders becomes domesticated, adjusted to the realities of the contemporary world. Succeeding generations do not dream the same dream. Momentum is lost and the congregation cares less about risking itself for the future and more about preserving its life in the present.

From my observations it seems that a common vision often begins in a personal way, with a pastor who has vision and is able to communicate that vision to his or her congregation. I never cease to be amazed at congregations who will enthusiastically and valiantly follow a pastor into the most unlikely places simply because they have sensed and collectively affirmed the pastor's own vision—so hungry are people for someone who has a vision of something. Allegiance to a visionary pastor has its own inherent dangers, which will be mentioned later, but, for now, let us simply note that the pastor's own sense of vision is crucially important in the formation of a congregation's sense of direction and vision.

Common Shared Life Together

A congregation must share the intimacy, relatedness, and mutual feeling that is the visible sign to the world of the presence of the realm of God in our midst. Just before he died, Paul Tillich noted that whereas the theology of the 1950s and 1960s was concerned with questions of reconciliation and estrangement, the theology of the 1970s and 1980s would be primarily concerned with questions of meaning and community. Although we have noted that the mere presence of congregational "friendliness" (real or imagined) is not, in itself, a guarantee that the congregation is a specifically *Christian* congregation, it is interesting that many people join churches and many remain in churches because of a congregation's alleged friendliness. The United States is caught between its strong individualism, its fragmented "pursuit of loneliness,"[3] and a deep yearning for togetherness, unity, and community. There can be no doubt that many people join a church primarily because they are lonely, fragmented, and yearning to be part of a group that cares—regardless of that group's theological commitments or lack of them.

But people who expect churches to be friendly, intimate, caring, unified, and cohesive also are recognizing an essential element of a Christian church. A Christian church, by the very nature of its vocation, vision, mandate, and promise, is expected to demonstrate a life together that witnesses to the love of the gospel itself. From the beginning of the church, a proof that the church was of divine origin and substance was that outsiders looked at the church and exclaimed, "See how they love one another."

In recent years many progressive congregations have put great stress on congregational involvement in the needs of the surrounding community. Some of these churches have defined themselves as "servants of the community" and have put much energy into community outreach: day-care centers, senior citizens' centers, boy and girl scouts, and recreational facilities for the community. All this activity may be admirable work for a church—but not at the expense of its own internal needs. This is not to say that a congregation cannot serve its own need for unity, fellowship, care of its members, internal maintenance and growth, and, at the same time, serve the community. It is to say that a congregation that neglects its own internal needs is unlikely to offer much substantial outreach.

Many pastors believe that the "action" in ministry is anywhere but among the priesthood of the local congregation. They therefore invest themselves in work with community social agencies, service clubs, government programs, and other activities outside the church. One suspects that some pastors involve themselves in community concerns because such abstracted, free-floating involvement is safer and easier than serious engagement with the needs, difficulties, conflicts, and hurts within the congregation itself. Once again, this is not to say that a church should not be engaged in work "in the world." (In fact, the next unifying factor is "Common Shared Life in the World.") I am simply saying that there is unlikely to be significant outreach or concern for the "world" until the "world" that gathers within the congregation experiences someone reaching out and concerned about it within the congregation itself. As someone said recently, we have spent too much time talking about the need for the church to serve the community when we also should have been talking about the necessity of building a community within the church.

In a congregation that enjoys a common shared life together, everyone is on a first-name basis. Members enjoy being with one another. All know and are known. The congregation has a healthy ability to mobilize to meet the needs of one of its members who experiences some acute crisis. When one suffers, all suffer. When one rejoices, all rejoice. Members speak most often in terms of "we" and "ours" rather than "me" and "mine." There is a sense of shared responsibility for the weaker members of the congregation: the poor, the infirm, the old, and the young. Usually, there is a fair amount of infighting and bickering in a congregation, which shows a firm sense of common shared life together. A closely unified congregation loves like a family and fights like a family. Intimacy, in families or in congregations, can lead to conflict. Sometimes members are so close, so continually close, that they know all too well one another's strengths and weaknesses. But the conflict can be productive. At least people

117

care enough to fight! In times of conflict the pastor plays the role of arbitrator or referee, rather than the one who urges people to supress their feelings. The pastor can help to assure people that the faith community has the resources to move through conflict to a workable resolution.[4]

Anthropologist Victor Turner said that "*communitas* is a gift to those who are willing to share the ordeal of liminality."[5] In other words, unity and community are given only to those who are able to risk close encounter with the boundaries and limits of life. Only the congregation that is willing to confront the boundaries of life and death, joy and sorrow, consensus and conflict, belief and doubt can achieve deep and lasting unity. This is why congregational difficulties, such as the loss of a pastor, or the building of a new church, or controversial political involvement can have the effect of a rite of passage, an ordeal through which the congregation moves to a deeper sense of community. We must never forget that a church is more a family than a formal organization. Whenever we look on congregations as mere administrative entities, as branch offices for the denomination's programs, we have misread how congregations view themselves. Whenever a pastor tries to administer or manage a congregation as if it were a business or social service agency, the pastor will be frustrated by the congregation's sense that it is called for a life together that is more familial than administrative.

Some may say that conceiving of a church as a family is only a romantic, nostalgic yearning for a social construction of the past that cannot function in today's world. I disagree. In a world where people increasingly structure their lives by the balancing of the competing self-interest and a series of short-term contractual associations, the need for a family-type association may be more strongly felt than ever before. Perhaps we avoid the intimacy of the family because so close a bond is risky to our overblown individualism. The family-like congregation requires an emotional and intellectual investment of us that is unlike the safer confines of the short-term association. So we keep everything neat, contractual, carefully balanced, and aloof, lest we lose our individuality within something that transcends us. The local congregation, by its very existence, is a protest against the isolation and alienation that accompany most of our modern associations.[6]

Admittedly, the various characteristics of a common shared life together (everyone knowing everyone else on a first-name basis, a common sense of responsibility and care, and a firm sense of belonging) suggest a rather small, intimate, family-like congregation. Large congregations have serious problems when it comes to fulfilling their vocations as locations for common shared life together. Large congregations must be more intentional about their life together than smaller congregations. Congregationally, the question might be raised: Is it possible, or desirable, to form congregations that are numerically too large to achieve the kind of unity and intimacy being advocated here?[7]

Common Shared Life in the World

A Christian congregation is called to be more than an isolated enclave of like-minded friends. A church is also called to be a visible witness to the ever coming realm of God in the world. When congregational togetherness becomes narcissistic self-infatuation, something is wrong. The church exists between the tension of being not of the world and yet also called to win and transform the world. Unfortunately, in recent years, many have come to believe that a concern for congregational unity and cohesiveness is antithetical to a concern to reach and serve the world. Congregations who take congregational unity with great seriousness are accused of being turned in on themselves, indifferent to the needs and hurts of the world around them, self-centered and self-concerned. This is a false dichotomy. A congregation must love itself before it is capable of loving others. A congregation will not love its neighbors in a vibrant, committed way until it has first learned to love its own witness, its own tradition, its own message, its own life together. A congregation must first be confident and optimistic about itself before it will be motivated to share itself with the world. In fact, before it experiences the gospel within its own congregational life, a congregation has little gospel to share with anyone else.

In other words, I have saved "Common Shared Life in the World" until last in order to stress that this unifying factor is greatly dependent on all the preceding factors. The church, like Jesus, is called to be about God's business. But all business is not Christian business. Too many churches have, of late, let "the world set the agenda," without asking about the purpose of the meeting. They have involved themselves in an endless round of activities, proclaimed themselves to be the "full-program church" with day-care centers, basketball teams, senior citizen's recreation, political action, etc. All this may be worthwhile activity for the church. But it may also be meaningless activity of a congregation that, having lost the theological focus and purpose of its life, now seeks to justify its existence by being "useful"—as the secular society judges usefulness. No activity, however useful or kind it may appear to be, is specifically Christian activity unless it is authorized and judged by a specifically Christian understanding of service to the world.

A congregation's investment in the needs of the world can confirm or foster a new sense of congregational identity and unity. Some congregations may discover what it means to be *Christian* congregations through praxis, by actually trying to live as Christians in the world. Investment in the world may force a congregation to define who it is and why it is in the world in a way that would not have been necessary if the congregation had remained within the cozy confines of its own life together.

Even when that involvement brings conflict, a congregation's response to the conflict can promote a more unified body. The conflict can provide an occasion for the working through of a congregation's identity and faith. Someone will say, "Remember the time we all got together and stopped the new freeway through the neighborhood?" This time of congregational commitment, risk, and involvement had become part of the congregation's memory, a warmly remembered moment when the congregation experienced itself not only as a unified group, but also as a visible witness to the reign of God in the world.

Having noted six requisites for the unity of a congregation, let me examine a few major ways in which, through his or her priestly work, the "community person" helps to create community in the congregation. Community is usually the by-product rather than the goal of these activities. But without these activities, community would be difficult, if not impossible, to achieve.

Achieving Unity in the Congregation's Day-to-Day Life

The purpose of Christian worship is the praise and enjoyment of God and nothing else. Whenever worship is used for human purposes, even for the most noble of human purposes, it is being used and thereby abused. Worship is directed toward God, not toward the mere fulfillment of human needs—other than that human need to praise and enjoy God. However, while we are praising and enjoying God, we find the human needs are met. Edification, education, hope, warmth, assurance, and peace can be by-products of worship. Community is one of the significant by-products of corporate worship.[8]

While any service of congregational worship can be an important source of congregational unity, I will focus on the ritual dimensions of two primary types of services that anthropologists call rites of initiation (i.e., baptism) and rites of intensification (i.e., Sunday morning worship).

Ritual is patterned, purposeful, predictable behavior that a group follows on a periodic basis. Unfortunately, liberal Protestantism has put more emphasis on ideas, words, and individualized action than on intuitive, emotional, corporate action. We have stressed social action over corporate, symbolic, communal action, forgetting that ritual is necessary to support significant social action over time. Ritual orders experience, provides meanings through symbolic actions that plumb the depths of crisis by carrying us through life's crises. Through our rituals we act out new patterns of behavior, we make believe that we are other than ourselves, thus acting out and experimenting with new patterns of behavior before we actually adopt the behavior.

Ritual is a powerful determinant of unity and community. Every cohesive human society lives by its rituals. In ritual we experience a oneness with others, a common tradition, and common values. Rituals are primary ways of establishing contact with the community's tradition, maintaining continuity with the past, and repeating a community's vision for the future. The question for the church is not "Will we live by ritual?" The question is "Will our rituals adequately express our faith and form our community as a specifically Christian community?" The pastor or priest is a sort of ritual specialist within the congregation, constantly evaluating the effectiveness and faithfulness of the church's rituals.

Rites of Initiation

Anthropologists have identified a series of ritual actions that result in decisive changes of a person's status and role—rites of initiation. Through a series of ordeals, people learn the ways and understandings of a community and are thereby transformed from isolated individuals into functioning members of the community. Elaborate incorporation rites, by which Christians become members of the church, were characteristic of the first four centuries of the Christian era. These rites were designed to foster a profound change in the life of the initiate through a long process of instruction, moral change, and personal ordeal. The assumption behind these rites of initiation was that one could not be born a Christian— one had to be made into a Christian. Baptism is the rite of Christian initiation. The church has been given the mandate to "make disciples" by "baptizing" and "teaching" (Matthew 28:19–20). The traditional goal of baptism is full incorporation into the church. The assumption behind the early rites of initiation was that one could not be a Christian withhout a careful, demanding, long-term process of conversion and nurture. As Mircea Eliade notes, initiation rites, in all religions, are "equivalent to a basic change in existential condition: The novice emerges from his ordeal with a totally different being from that which he possessed before his initiation; he has become another."[9]

The conversion of Christians was never regarded as a once-and-for-all rite. Baptism itself was only part of a long process of initiation. One became Christian only after a complex series of rituals. A unified, cohesive congregation takes its formal and informal rites of initiation seriously. Anthropologists identify three parts of a rite of initiation.

Separation. The initiate is separated symbolically from his or her old state of being. In so-called primitive societies adolescents who are being initiated into adulthood are sent into the jungle for a long period of withdrawal. During this time elders in the tribe instruct the youth in the skills and knowledge of the tribe. Most churches have short periods of separation, if any. Some pastors form an "Inquirers' Class" for all older youth and adults who wish to join the congregation. Inquirers are set apart from the congregation and designated as subjects of special care and instruction.

Transition. The initiate is placed in a state of flux—"betwixt and between," as Victor Turner calls it.[10] In this phase of the rite of initiation, the initiate experiences what Turner calls "liminality"; that is, the initiate has begun to move toward the community but is not yet fully within the community. This state is equivalent to the engagement period before marriage. In the congregation, candidates participate in the congregation's worship, but they do not yet fully understand the meaning of that worship. They know a few persons, such as the pastor or their sponsors, but they do not yet know all the people. The transition stage is the time for education, self-examination, and examination by the congregation.

All rites of initiation, during their separation and transition phases, are experienced as an ordeal, a passageway that the initiate is required to go through before being admitted to the new state of existence. The more arduous the ordeal, the more expectant and committed the candidates. When candidates become members, their commitment is almost in exact proportion to the difficulty of the ordeal they went through to become members.

Incorporation. During this final stage the individual is received into the group. The initiate comes in with the confidence that he or she has received the skills and information one needs for full participation and identification with the group. Although a service that is part of the rite of initiation will often encapsulate or recapitulate all three phases of the rite of initiation, the service will usually take place as the culmination of a candidate's incorporation.

Baptism is the rite of Christian initiation. Baptism makes someone a member of the family of God and incorporates the initiate, the baptized, into the Body of Christ. Unfortunately, entrance into most congregations is something less than rigorous. Too often initiation is merely "joining the church," voluntary institutional affiliation that demands little change or commitment on the part of the initiate, or little acceptance and incorporation on the part of the congregation. The formal and informal rituals are done in a haphazard, unintentional way. The products of such casual initiation reveal the same casualness in their church membership. Anthropologists say that a breakdown of initiation rites usually denotes a breakdown of the community or, conversely, a breakdown of the community is often preceded by a breakdown of the community's initiation rites.

One of the fascinating things about the Christian church, in its first three centuries, is that during a time of persecution and a fight for its very life, the church, rather than enthusiastically welcoming all comers, built walls around itself. The church was careful to differentiate between insiders and outsiders, insisting on a rigorous change of life-style and disposition of all who would enter. A three-year adult catechumenate was the norm in the early Roman church.

Across the American church we need to give serious attention to our rites of Christian initiation. In a strict sense one cannot "join" a unified, cohesive congregation because, as argued earlier, a unified congregation is best conceived of as a family. One can only be adopted into a family. One can seek membership, but membership is, finally, a gift. Throughout my own denomination I have seen congregations that are virtually closed to outsiders because they have no way of seeking and integrating outsiders. Congregational unity has become dysfunctional, closed, and potentially self-destructive. Other congregations regularly attract and receive new members but fail to integrate these newcomers. The lack of functional rites of initiation is testimony to the lack of identity within the congregation, which only aggravates the diffuse, fragmented quality of congregational life. People do not wish to affiliate with a society having so little self-respect that no process of initiation is necessary. Failing truly to initiate new life into the congregation, the congregation finds that new members become divisive factors within the congregation, troublesome newcomers who attempt to force a congregation to bow to their individual expectations, since the congregation has neglected to initiate and integrate newcomers into a congregation's shared expectations.

Rites of Intensification

Another major group of rituals are periodic ceremonials relating to the life of a group and its shared beliefs and symbols. These rituals are called rites of intensification. Through these cyclic rites a group intensifies commitment to its particular set of meanings and values, individuals in the group continue to be habituated to the patterned behavior of the group, a network of relationships is forged among participants, and common loyalties are passed on to the young and reinforced among the old.[11] Rites of intensification invariably recount important traditions and myths. These help to maintain group cohesiveness as well as to judge the present form of the group.

Rites of intensification have an inherently conservative quality about them. They are dealing with sacred history. But it is not history as a dead relic from the past; it is history as determinative of who the group is today and where the group ought to be going in the future. The remembrance that occurs in these periodic rites is waking up, rediscovering who the group is now. It is history remembered, not as a set of dates and names, but rather as history that is experienced, embodied in the behavior of the participants in the rite.[12] Meanings become concrete, alive, intense, and compelling through the drama for the ritual and are given permanence through repetition. The Christian eucharist or Holy Communion, at which the pastor presides as priest, is a typical rite of intensification—an active "remembrance" of the identity, the past, present, and future of the Christian community.[13]

Every time the congregation gathers on Sunday morning it is experiencing a rite of intensification, rehearsing its sacred history, recapitulating its past, affirming its beliefs, and acting

126

out the essential features of who it's supposed to be. Every Sunday service can be a powerful (and too often overlooked) source of community formation. Historically, the Sunday service was the primary occasion in congregational life for Christian education and nurture, initiation of new members, pastoral care, evangelism, and witness. Modern congregations may need to ask themselves questions like: Is the Christian story being told in its fullness and completeness on Sunday morning? Are we adequately rehearsing and passing on our shared meanings and traditions to our young? Can people be full participants in the community's life without participating in the community's worship?

Implications for Contemporary Ministry

As the ordained ministry emerged in the first centuries of the church, congregations designated people to lead in their worship and in their life together. Some scholars believe that two basic patterns of ministry eventually merged. In Jewish Christian congregations a pattern of leadership was adopted from the synagogue. A group of "elders" *(presbuteroi)* ruled the congregation. Certain elders were designated to lead worship, others to oversee congregational welfare and teach new converts. In Gentile Christian congregations, however, one person was designated to lead. This person was called the "bishop," or "superintendent" *(episkopos)*. In these congregations the bishop was the pastor of an individual congregation. Often the bishop would designate members of the congregation to serve as assistants. These assistants were called "deacons" *(diakonoi)*. By the third century these two forms of leadership merged in the Western church. A bishop was elected by the congregation's elders. The bishop was assisted in this work by deacons. The bishop's main functions were to preside at the eucharist and conduct catechesis. The deacons assisted the bishop at the eucharist and helped oversee the church's work among widows and orphans. Elders oversaw the governance and discipline of the congregation. After the fourth century a number of congregations in a designated geographical area were placed under the control of a bishop so that a bishop was no longer tied to an individual congregation. Individual congregations came under the control of a single elder. This is the origin of what became the monarchical episcopacy and the hierarchical priesthood.

Thus, probably by the end of the first century, and certainly by the late second century, the church found it helpful to set apart some Christians for the task of leading, edifying, and unifying the congregation. All Christians were "ordained" to participate in Christ's ministry to the world by virtue of their baptism. But, from the beginning, some Christians were given the additional burden of edifying a congregation. Behind our attempt to reconstruct the history of the ordained ministry is the truth that ministry arose, in the words of Edward Schillebeeckx, "from below," from the Christian community's need for leadership. At the same time leadership in the church is "from above," in that the church sees its unity and its leaders as gifts of the Lord (Ephesians 4:8–11; 1 Timothy 4:14, 2 Timothy 1:6).[14]

As stated at the beginning, the special thing about ordained ministers is not their possession of some special *character indelibilis*, or some other characteristic that detaches their authority from the community. The special thing about ordained ministers is that they are "community people."

> The priest from earliest times of the church was the one designated by the community to share and represent Christ's community-wide vision. The concentration of the priest is upon the community-forming as well as community criticizing dimensions of the faith; . . . edification is the burden of his or her particular vocation to the ministry. The pastor is the one who is charged with seeing . . . individual lives within the context of the whole; to bear the sometimes heavy burden of the community's tradition; to note the presence of inequality, division, and diversity; to create the conditions necessary for consensus;

to foster a climate where reconciliation can occur; to judge the potentially demonic aspects of our "togetherness"; to ask whether the community we seek and attain is a specifically Christian community; to distinguish between his or her personal preferences and what community cohesion, maintenance, and critique require.[15]

What strikes one in looking at the witness of the church is the wisdom it showed in choosing to focus its identity, vision, and authority on a person. Perhaps this is because the gospel itself is intensely personal. The gospel is not so much a new idea or even a new life-style. It is a person, the person to whom we persons are called to give our lives. The presence of Christ, "where two or three are gathered together," is intensely personal.

Pastors promote unity within a congregation as a representative, a symbol of the life and identity of the entire congregation, indeed of the church universal. When the pastor is present during times of individual need or crisis in the wider community, "we" are there too. The pastor represents the congregation, not because members of the congregation are incompetent to do the things a pastor does. By their baptism the laity also have a ministry, including many "priestly" activities of the church. Contemporary liturgical and congregational renewal has taken 1 Peter 2:9 as its scriptural model: "But you are a chosen race, a royal priesthood, a holy nation, God's own people, that you may declare the wonderful deeds of him who called you out of darkness into his marvelous light." The congregation is itself the "royal priesthood," the body from which the pastor's priestly functions are derived.

Since Vatican Council II, for instance, certain laypersons are designated as "Lay Ministers of the Eucharist," making them active ministers of a function that had been designated for the priest alone. In many parishes the laity may assist in the leadership of parts of the Sunday liturgy. Even the homily may be delivered by a layperson in Catholic churches, depending on the texts for the day, the occasion, and the talent within the congregation. In so doing the church reminds itself that the whole church is a royal priesthood.

From out of this shared priesthood the pastor is the designated official of the church, the "community person," whose officialness is recognized by the members on a continuing basis. The legitimacy of the clergy is principally in its ability to awaken the baptismally bestowed ministry of all Christians. The need for clergy is not only sociologically understandable, but also historically defensible. Recent attempts to define a pastor as an "enabler" of the laity, or as a congregational manager who stands in the wings and coordinates everyone else's ministry, do not do justice either to the historic bases for the ordained ministry or to a group's legitimate leadership needs. A pastor represents not only the needs and aspirations of the individual congregation, but also the tradition, memory, vision, and standards of the universal church in a way that is neither expected nor possible for all Christians in general. It is inconceivable that there could be a dynamic, committed ministry of the laity that is not led by the dynamic, committed ministry of a pastor. The pastor is, to use an old term for church officials, a *ponte fex* (literally, "bridge builder") for the congregation, the one who is constantly building bridges between rich and poor, young and old, newcomers and old-timers, insiders and outsiders in the congregation.

Having spoken of the pastor as a force for unity in the congregation by virtue of his or her representative function, some may wonder how such pastoral leadership avoids becoming a mere "personality cult," a demonic, clericalized, individualized, self-aggrandizing style of leadership that can be the death of a vibrant lay ministry. Admittedly, the church has a long history of problems with its leaders, particularly when its leaders forget that they are "community people" and seek a more self-legitimated, self-serving role in the church. While not denying the danger of the church degenerating into a personality cult for the pastor rather than the Body of Christ, I

130

think a couple of observations need to be made about this problem.

First, pastoral leadership is utterly essential and frighteningly determinative for the life of a unified congregation. After observing a number of churches that appear to be working as opposed to churches that do not appear to be working, I am forced to make this conclusion: When one isolates all the factors that make or break a congregation, pastoral leadership is always at the top of the list. We pastors often overestimate the importance of the theological stance of the leader, the social context of the congregation, or the quality of indigenous lay leadership. (Perhaps we overestimate these factors in an attempt to remove the leadership burden from our shoulders!) In the churches I have observed, it is as if all things can be overcome or rendered irrelevant by a skillful, caring, competent pastor, whose ministry is so visible as to awaken ministry in everyone else in the congregation. In receiving ministry from another, ministry is awakened in each of us. The pastor is concerned to foster unity and cohesion within the congregation so that it might have the strength and vision to be the priestly people we are called to be.

Unfortunately, some in the church have tried to build up the "ministry of the laity" by downgrading the importance of the ministry of the pastor. But the "priesthood of all believers" doctrine does not eliminate the necessity of priests. Whatever dangers there are in the "personality cult" style of pastoral leadership, these dangers must not be overcome by simply doing away with leaders. To do so makes the church vulnerable to even greater dangers.

Second, having affirmed the necessity of strong pastoral leadership in a congregation, I want to consider under what conditions pastoral leadership sometimes degenerates into a self-centered "personality cult" for the pastor. It appears that personality cults develop most often in the absence of the six factors I listed for a unified congregation. When a congregation lacks a common sense of identity, a common authority, a common memory, a common vision, a common shared life together, and a common shared life in the world, it must seek its identity, its vision, its unity elsewhere. Too often the pastor becomes the surrogate source of a congregation's unity. The congregation becomes "the Rev. Smith's church" and envisions itself as rallying around a beloved or charismatic personality. The pastor stops being the "community person" and becomes the "superapostle" (as Paul called them in 2 Corinthians 11:5), the superdoer of good works, the superattractive pulpit star.

The way to avoid such perversion of ministry is not to destroy the pastoral ministry. Priests can be a source of authority for the congregation without being authoritarian by never forgetting that they are community persons, that they stand, with the community, under the identity, authority, memory, vision, and mission of the one who judges and forgives the priest, along with the community the priest is called to serve: "In every way into him who is the head, into Christ, from whom the whole body, joined and knit together by every joint with which it is supplied, when each part is working properly, makes bodily growth and upbuilds itself in love [Eph. 4:15–16]."

Having begun with baptismal imagery in Ephesians 4:4–6, this segment of Ephesians ends the thoughts on the priestly task of creating community by returning to baptism as the source of Christian unity. The growth of the whole community is being stressed here, not individual members. "Joined and knit together [4:16]" suggests the baptismal image of the initiate being joined to Christ, grafted to the church, part of the Body. By water and the Spirit it is the priest's burden and privilege to be part of this growing, strengthening love.

Notes

Introduction

1. Cf. W.A. Visser 't Hooft, *The Kingship of Christ* (New York: Harper & Brothers, 1948), p. 15; and George H. Tavard, *A Theology for Ministry* (Wilmington, DE: Michael Glazier, 1983), pp. 127–28.
2. For more extensive discussions of titles attributed to or conferred on Jesus and their theological and Christological implications see, for example, Ferdinand Hahn, *The Titles of Jesus in Christology* (New York: World Publishing Co., 1969), and R.H. Fuller, *The Foundations of New Testament Christology* (New York: Charles Scribner's Sons, 1965).
3. Cf. Earl E. Shelp and Ronald H. Sunderland, eds., *The Pastor as Prophet* (New York: The Pilgrim Press, 1985).
4. Cf. Earl E. Shelp and Ronald H. Sunderland, eds., *The Pastor as Servant* (New York: The Pilgrim Press, 1986).
5. John Calvin, *Institutes of the Christian Religion*, Bk. II, ch. 15, *Library of Christian Classics*, vol. 20, ed. John T. McNeill (Philadelphia: Westminster Press, 1960), p. 502.
6. M.H. Shepherd Jr., "Priests in the NT," *Interpreter's Dictionary of the Bible*, vol. 2 (Nashville, TN: Abingdon Press, 1962), p. 890.
7. Lesslie Newbigin, "Four Talks on I Peter," *We Were Brought Together*, ed. David M. Taylor (Sidney: Australian Council for the World Council of Churches, 1960), p. 97.
8. Ibid., p. 98.
9. James A. Wharton, "Theology and Ministry in the Hebrew Scriptures," *A Biblical Basis for Ministry*, ed. Earl E. Shelp and Ronald H. Sunderland (Philadelphia: Westminster Press, 1981), p. 47.

Chapter 1. The Ministry as Function and Being

1. See George H. Tavard, "The Meaning of Melchizedek for Contemporary Ministry," chapter 4 in this volume.

2. The consistency and basic consensus of many churches on the continuity of Christ's ministry in the churches' ministries is thoroughly documented. Important citations are as follows: *The Third World Conference on Faith and Order,* Lund, 1952, ed. O. S. Tomkins (London: SCM Press, 1953), p. 24; *The Fourth World Conference on Faith and Order,* Montreal, 1963, ed. P. C. Rodger and L. Vischer (New York: Association Press, 1964), p. 64. The bilateral reports and agreed statements of churches at the world level reveal the convergence, especially in the book *Growth in Agreement,* ed. Harding Meyer and Lukas Vischer (New York: Paulist Press, 1984). Citations of Anglicans, Lutherans, Orthodox, Baptists, Reformed, Methodists, and Roman Catholics are found on pp. 24, 45, 82–83, 149, 182, 253, 328, 456.

3. *Fourth World Conference on Faith and Order,* p. 64.

4. George H. Tavard provides a needed warning against schematizing the "Three Offices" of Christ, a concept of ancient origin. Jesus' ministry is characterized in the New Testament by several other titles and metaphors. Cf. *A Theology for Ministry* (Wilmington, DE: Michael Glazier, 1983), p. 127.

5. E.O. James, *The Nature and Function of Priesthood* (London: Thames and Hudson, 1955), pp. 277–99.

6. See Gerald F. Moede, "Priest and Pastor: Lessons from Our Predecessors," chapter 2 in this volume.

7. Bernard Cooke, *Ministry to Word and Sacraments* (Philadelphia: Fortress Press, 1976), p. 542.

8. John McKenzie, "Ministerial Structures in the New Testament," in *The Plurality of Ministries,* ed. Hans Kung and Walter Kasper (New York: Herder & Herder, 1972), p. 14.

9. Quoted in *An Invitation to Action: The Lutheran-Reformed Dialogue, Series III,* ed. James E. Andrews and Joseph A. Burgess (Philadelphia: Fortress Press, 1984), p. 35.

10. Roland H. Bainton, *Here I Stand* (New York: Abingdon-Cokesbury, 1940), p. 261.

11. See the important interpretation of "Scripture, Tradition and

Traditions" in *Fourth World Conference on Faith and Order,* pp. 50-61; Albert C. Outler, *The Christian Tradition and the Unity We Seek* (New York: Oxford University Press, 1957).

12. The Roman Catholic Church's recovery and acceptance of the priesthood of all believers is amply illustrated in recent literature, of which a few notable examples may be cited. Yves M. J. Congar, *Lay People in the Church* (London: Geoffrey Chapman, 1959); Congar's student, now a cardinal, Jerome Hamer, *The Church in a Communion* (New York: Sheed & Ward, 1964), pp. 101–10; Hans Kung, *Structures of the Church* (New York: Thomas Nelson & Sons, 1964), p. 94; *The Constitution on the Church (Lumen Gentium),* ch. 4, "The Laity," in *Documents of Vatican II,* ed. Walter M. Abbott (New York: Herder & Herder, 1966).

13. Karl Barth, *Church Dogmatics,* IV, pt. I (Edinburgh: T.&T. Clark, 1956), p. 666. This great modern reformed theologian repeats an insight of medieval Roman Catholic theologians. "As William of St. Thierry explains it in his *De sacramentis altaris,* the historical body, the sacramental body (often called the mystical body) and the ecclesial body are not three bodies but three modes of contemplation of the one body of Christ." Cf. Tavard, *A Theology for Ministry,* p. 36.

14. J. Ernest Rattenbury, *The Eucharistic Hymns of John and Charles Wesley* (London: Epworth Press, 1948), pp. 131, 239.

15. *Consultation on Church Union Consensus* (Princeton, NJ, 1985), p. 46.

16. *Baptism, Eucharist, and Ministry* (Geneva: World Council of Churches, 1982), p. 22.

17. Cooke, p. 543.

18. Despite recent bilateral agreements of Anglican and Roman Catholic theologians on the theology of ordination, the Anglican orders remain under the excluding ban of Pope Leo XIII's encyclical, *Apostolicae Curae,* 1896.

Chapter 2. Priest and Pastor: Lessons from Our Predecessors

1. Raymond Brown, *Priest and Bishop* (New York: Paulist Press, 1970), p. 13.

2. John McKenzie, *The Plurality of Ministries* (New York: Herder & Herder, 1972), p. 19.
3. Ronald E. Osborn, *In Christ's Place* (St. Louis: Bethany Press, 1967), p. 147.
4. Ibid., p. 153.
5. Massey H. Shepherd Jr., "Presbyters in the Early Church," *To Be a Priest*, ed. Robert E. Terwilliger and Urban T. Holmes III (New York: Seabury Press, 1975), p. 72.
6. Edward Schillebeeckx, *Ministry* (New York: Crossroads, 1981), p. 15.
7. Ibid., p. 29.
8. Hans Kung, *The Church* (New York: Sheed & Ward, 1967), p. 369.
9. Bernard Cooke, *Ministry to Word and Sacraments* (Philadelphia: Fortress Press, 1976), p. 539.
10. Ibid., p. 541.
11. Ibid.
12. Schillebeeckx, p. 49.
13. Cooke, p. 542.
14. Louis Weil, "Priesthood in the New Testament," in *To Be a Priest*, p. 75.
15. Cooke, p. 338.
16. Ibid., p. 555.
17. Ibid., p. 541.
18. Ibid., p. 550.
19. Ibid., p. 542.
20. Ibid., p. 561.
21. Weil, p. 64.
22. Schillebeeckx, p. 56.
23. Cooke, p. 556.
24. Ibid., p. 564.
25. Schillebeeckx, pp. 66–67.
26. Kasper, in *Plurality of Ministries*, p. 118.
27. Cooke, p. 147.
28. Edmund Schlink, *Theology of the Lutheran Confessions* (Philadelphia: Muhlenberg Press, 1960), pp. 238–51.
29. John Wesley, "Caution Against Bigotry," *John Wesley's 53 Sermons*, ed. Edward H. Sugden (Nashville, TN: Abingdon Press, 1983), p. 485.
30. Wesley, *Letters* II, pp. 55–56.

31. Albert Outler, "Do Methodists Have a Doctrine of the Church?" *The Doctrine of the Church*, ed. Dow Kirkpatrick (Nashville, TN: Abingdon Press, 1964), pp. 26–27.
32. Robert S. Michaelsen, "The Protestant Ministry in America: 1850 to Present," in *The Ministry in Historical Perspectives*, ed. H. Richard Niebuhr and Daniel D. Williams (New York: Harper & Brothers, 1956), p. 283.
33. Ibid.
34. Ibid.
35. Ibid.
36. Edward R. Hardy Jr., "Priestly Ministries in the Modern Church," in *Ministry in Historical Perspectives*, p. 175.
37. Ibid., p. 171.
38. Paul Minear, *Images of the Church in the New Testament* (Philadelphia: Westminster Press, 1960), p. 87.
39. John F. Jansen, "The Pastoral Image in the New Testament," *Austin Seminary Bulletin* 94 (May 1979): 15.
40. Cooke, p. 344.
41. Ibid., p. 345.
42. Schillebeeckx, p. 29.
43. United Methodist/Roman Catholic Statement: *Eucharistic Celebration: Converging Theology—Divergent Practice* MSS, 1981, pp. 10, 11.
44. C. FitzSimmons Allison, "Another Anglican View," in *To Be a Priest*, p. 13.
45. Ibid.
46. Osborn, p. 157.
47. Urban T. Holmes III, *The Future Shape of Ministry* (New York: Seabury Press, 1971), p. 27.
48. Cooke, p. 644.
49. *Baptism, Eucharist, and Ministry* (Geneva: World Council of Churches, 1982), p. 11.
50. Holmes, p. 96.
51. Robert Paul, *Ministry* (Grand Rapids, MI: Eerdmans, 1965), 37.
52. Osborn, p. 166.

Chapter 3. The Priestly Authority of Paul

1. Ralph P. Martin, *2 Corinthians, Word Biblical Commentary* (Waco, TX: Word Books, 1986), pp. 326–424.
2. For archaeological details, see the first two issues of *Biblical Archaeological Review*, 1986.
3. David Flusser, *Jesus*, tr. Ronald Walls (New York: Herder & Herder, 1969), p. 122.
4. Paul I. Murphy with R. Rene Arlington, *La Popessa* (New York: Warner Books, 1985). I owe this reference to Helen Ruchti, who was, for many years in Rome, a Priscilla with her husband, William C. Ruchti.
5. The quotation from the pamphlet is taken from Ira (Jack) Birdwhistell, *The Baptists of the Bluegrass* (Berea, KY: Berea College Press, 1985), p. 48.
6. Oscar Cullmann, *Message to Catholics and Protestants*, tr. Joseph A. Burgess (Grand Rapids, MI: Eerdmans, 1959).
7. Keith F. Nickle, *The Collection: A Study in Paul's Strategy* (Naperville, IL: Alec E. Allenson, 1966).
8. James Denny, *Word Pictures in the New Testament*, IV (Nashville, TN: Sunday School Board [of the Southern Baptist Convention], 1931), p. 420.
9. For a similar view and a careful evaluation of this post-Rome evidence, see Jack Finegan, *The Archeology of the New Testament, II: The Mediterranean World of the Early Christian Apostles* (Boulder, CO: Westview Press, 1981), pp. 34–39, 217–34. Finegan refers to my paper on "A New Chronology for the Life and Letters of Paul" on p. 237, note 17. The paper has now been reprinted several times, first in *Perspectives in Religious Studies* 3 (Fall 1976):248–71. See also "A New Chronology for the New Testament," *Review and Expositor*, Spring 1981, pp. 211–31.
10. Ernst Lohmeyer, *Meyer Kommentar*, IX, ed. 8, 1928; cf. Gerald F. Hawthorne, *Philippians, Word Biblical Commentary* (Waco, TX: Word Books, 1985), pp. iiif.
11. Charles M. Nielsen, "The Status of Paul and His Letters in Colossians," *Perspectives in Religious Studies* 12 (Summer 1985):103–22.
12. A quick summary may be seen in *The New International Ver-*

sion Study Bible, p. 1836f. This will be scoffed at by those who have already denied Paul's six Pauline Epistles, but I predict that the time will come when many more New Testament scholars will see the arbitrary way so much of the New Testament is assigned to some Saint Unknown.

Chapter 4. The Meaning of Melchizedek for Contemporary Ministry

1. I have used several recent commentaries, especially C. Spicq, *L'epitre aux Hebreux* (Paris: Gabalda, 1977); Louis Dussaut, *Synopse structurelle de l'epitre aux Hebreux, approche d'analyse structurelle)* (Paris: Le Cerf, 1981).
2. Spicq, *L'epitre aux Hebreux,* pp. 118–19.
3. The Sadducees, claiming the priest Zadok as their ancestor (mentioned in 1 Chronicles 15:11, as having been appointed by David, along with others, to supervise the transfer of the Ark of the Covenant to Jerusalem), were wiped out as a caste by the destruction of the temple, where they had traditionally held positions of authority. Although their religious tenets placed them farther from Jesus and the early disciples than the Pharisees were, some may have turned eventually to the Christian movement.
4. Raymond Brown does not think that the community of the Letter to the Hebrews, which he locates in Rome, was made of converted priests; see Raymond Brown and John Meier, *Antioch and Rome: New Testament Cradles of Catholic Christianity* (New York: Paulist Press, 1983), pp. 142–51.
5. Rene Girard, *Violence and the Sacred* (Baltimore: Johns Hopkins University Press, 1979); Rene Girard, *Des choses cachees depuis la fondation du monde* (Paris: Grasset, 1978); Rene Girard, *Le bouc emissaire* (Paris: Grasset, 1982).
6. Tertullian introduced the discussion of Melchizedek (*Adversus Judaeos* 11, 13; 111, 1), but he simply made the point that Melchizedek was a priest long before Aaron. Augustine could also have known Ambrose's utilization of the image of Melchizedek in *De sacramentis* V, i, 1–3: Ambrose held that Melchizedek offered a sacrifice of bread and wine, cf. *Des*

sacraments. *Des mysteres*, Sources Chretiennes, vol. 25 (Paris: Le Cerf, 1961), p. 110.

7. David Torrance and Thomas F. Torrance, eds., *Calvin's Commentaries: The Epistle of Paul the Apostle to the Hebrews, and the First and Second Epistles of St. Peter* (Grand Rapids, MI: Eerdmans, 1963), p. 94; the next quotations are from John Calvin, *Commentaires sur l'ancien testament. Le livre de la Genese* (Geneva: Labor et Fides, 1961), pp. 220–21. According to Calvin, Melchizedek was, in his time, "the only head of the whole Church" (p. 220); Calvin renders *sacerdos* as "sacrificer" (*sacrificateur*).

8. One can refer to the major ecumenical documents on the eucharist and the priesthood, such as *Lutherans and Catholics in Dialogue* (USA), vol. 3; *The Eucharist as Sacrifice* (Washington, DC: USCC, 1967), vol. 4; *Eucharist and Ministry*, 1970; Lutheran/Roman Catholic Joint Commission (international), *The Eucharist* (Geneva: Lutheran World Federation, 1980); Anglican-Roman Catholic International Commission, *The Final Report* (London: SPCK, 1982); Faith and Order Commission, *Baptism, Eucharist, and Ministry* (Geneva: World Council of Churches, 1982). None uses the image of Melchizedek. For the broader ecumenical problem of ministry, see George H. Tavard, *A Theology for Ministry* (Wilmington, DE: Michael Glazier, 1983).

9. Rather than follow the text verse by verse, Luther's commentary on Hebrews examines only a number of selected questions. See *Luther's Works*, vol. 29, *Lectures on Titus, Philemon, and Hebrews* (St. Louis: Concordia, 1968), p. 192.

10. Tavard, *Theology for Ministry*.

Chapter 5. Antique Clothes and a Digital Watch

1. M. Helene Pollock, "Growing Toward Effective Ministry," *Women Ministers: How Women Are Redefining Traditional Roles*, ed. Judith L. Weidman (San Francisco: Harper & Row, 1981), p. 17.

2. In addition to books by the authors mentioned, several issues of *Concilium* have been devoted to aspects of this topic, among them *The Pastoral Mission of the Church*, vol. 3, ed. Karl

Rahner (Glen Rock, NJ: Paulist Press, 1965); *The Identity of the Priest*, vol. 43, ed. Karl Rahner (New York: Paulist Press, 1969); and *Women in a Men's Church*, ed. Virgil Elizondo and Norbert Greinacher (New York: Seabury Press, 1980). An additional, significant collection is *Official Ministry in a New Age*, ed. James H. Provost (Washington, DC: Canon Law Society of America, The Catholic University of America, 1981).

3. *Baptism, Eucharist, and Ministry*, Faith and Order Paper, 111 (Geneva: World Council of Churches, 1982). This document was approved at the Sixth Assembly of the World Council of Churches in Vancouver, British Columbia, in 1983 and is now circulated worldwide among the churches, asking them to respond to a series of questions including "To what extent can your church 'recognize in this text the faith of the Church through the ages'?" Hereafter this document will be referred to as BEM.

4. Major Roman Catholic works in this area include two books by Karl Rahner, *The Shape of the Church to Come* (London: SPCK, 1972) and *The Spirit in the Church* (New York: Seabury Press, 1979), and two volumes by Edward Schillebeeckx, *The Mission of the Church* (New York: Crossroad, 1985). Major Protestant works include Jurgen Moltmann, *The Church in the Power of the Spirit* (New York: Harper & Row, 1975), and Wolfhart Pannenberg, *The Church* (Philadelphia: Westminster Press, 1977).

5. Barbara Brown Zikmund, "Expanding Horizons: Coming to New Consciousness as a North American," *Changing Contexts of Our Faith*, ed. Letty M. Russell (Philadelphia: Fortress Press, 1985), p. 45.

6. The closest parallels to the BEM convergence texts would be the Klingenthal report of the World Council of Churches Community of Women and Men in the Church, *Ordination of Women in Ecumenical Perspective*, Faith and Order Paper, 105, ed. Constance F. Parvey (Geneva: World Council of Churches, 1980), and *The Community of Women and Men in the Church: The Sheffield Report*, ed. Constance F. Parvey (Philadelphia: Fortress Press, 1983).

7. Parvey, *The Sheffield Report*, p. 132.

8. BEM (paragraph 35), p. 29.

9. The literature of reconstruction of women's leadership roles in the church from apostolic times to the present is rich, ranging from popular books such as Elisabeth Moltmann-Wendel's, *The Women Around Jesus* (London: SCM Press, 1982) to Elisabeth Schussler Fiorenza's, *In Memory of Her* (New York: Crossroad, 1983). Among the recent studies of women in the High Middle Ages are Caroline Walker Bynum, *Jesus as Mother: Studies in the Spirituality of the High Middle Ages* (Berkeley: University of California Press, 1982); Clarissa W. Atkinson, *Mystic and Pilgrim: The Book and World of Margery Kempe* (Ithaca, NY: Cornell University Press, 1983); and Peter Dronke, *Women Writers of the Middle Ages* (Cambridge: Cambridge University Press, 1984).

10. Parvey, *The Sheffield Report*, p. 29.

11. Ibid., pp. 133–34.

12. Nelle Morton, *The Journey Is Home* (Boston: Beacon Press, 1985), pp. 202–3.

13. Leontine T. C. Kelly, "Preaching in the Black Tradition," in *Women Ministers*, p. 76.

14. BEM (paragraph 18), pp. 23–24.

15. BEM (paragraph 50), p. 32.

16. Una Kroll, *Flesh of My Flesh* (London: Darton, Longman & Todd, 1975), pp. 102–3.

17. BEM (paragraph 45), p. 31.

18. Fran Ferder, "Those Who Feel Called to Priesthood," in *New Woman, New Church, New Priestly Ministry* (Rochester, NY: Women's Ordination Conference, 1980), pp. 103–4.

19. Edward C. Lehman Jr., *Women Clergy: Breaking Through Gender Barriers* (New Brunswick, NJ: Transaction Books, 1985), p. 274.

20. BEM (paragraph 35), p. 29.

21. BEM (paragraph 39), p. 30.

22. BEM (paragraph 15), p. 22.

23. BEM (paragraph 16), p. 23.

24. Ada Maria Isasi-Diaz, "Toward an Understanding of *Feminismo Hispano* in the U.S.A.," *Women's Consciousness, Women's Conscience: A Reader in Feminist Ethics,* ed. Barbara Hilkert Andolsen, Christine E. Gudorf, and Mary D. Pellauer (Minneapolis: Winston Press, 1984), p. 53.

25. Karl Rahner, *The Shape of the Church to Come* (London: SPCK, 1974), p. 121.
26. BEM (paragraph 8), p. 21.
27. BEM (paragraph 42), p. 30.
28. Ibid.
29. Catherina Halkes, "Feminist Theology: An Interim Assessment," *Women in a Men's Church*, ed. Virgil Elizondo and Norbert Greinacher (New York: Seabury Press, 1980), pp. 117–18.

Chapter 6. The Priestly Task in Creating Community

1. Donald McGavran, *Understanding Church Growth* (Grand Rapids, MI: Eerdmans, 1970).
2. I thank my colleague John Westerhoff for helping me define these six requisites.
3. Philip Slater, *The Pursuit of Loneliness: American Society at the Breaking Point* (Boston: Beacon Press, 1970).
4. Paul A. Mickey and Robert L. Wilson, *Conflict and Resolution* (Nashville, TN: Abingdon Press, 1973).
5. Victor W. Turner, *The Ritual Process: Structure and Anti-Structure* (Chicago: Aldine, 1960).
6. Here I am building on the insights of Gregory Baum, *Alienation in Industrial Society: Ferdinand Toennies, Religion and Alienation* (Ramsey, NJ: Paulist Press, 1976).
7. See William H. Willimon and Robert L. Wilson, *Preaching and Worship in the Small Membership Church* (Nashville, TN: Abingdon Press, 1980).
8. William H. Willimon, "Liturgy and Community: The Lord's Supper," *Worship as Pastoral Care* (Nashville, TN: Abingdon Press, 1979), pp. 166–94.
9. Mircea Eliade, *Rites and Symbols of Initiation* (New York: Harper Torchbook, 1958), p. x.
10. Turner, pp. 153–60.
11. Peter L. Berger and Thomas Luckmann, *The Social Construction of Reality* (Garden City, NY: Doubleday, 1966), p. 158.
12. Edward Norbeck, *Religion in Primitive Society* (New York: Harper & Row, 1961), pp. 138ff.

13. Willimon, *Worship as Pastoral Care* (Nashville: Abingdon Press, 1979), pp. 174–94.
14. Edward Schillebeeckx, *Ministry: Leadership in the Community of Jesus Christ*, tr. John Bowden (New York: Crossroad, 1981), pp. 6–7.
15. Ibid., pp. 203–4.